The Promulgation of Law

THE CATHOLIC UNIVERSITY OF AMERICA
CANON LAW STUDIES
No. 241

THE PROMULGATION OF LAW

BY THE
REV. MARTIN NICHOLAS LOHMULLER, A.B., J.C.L.
Priest of the Archdiocese of Philadelphia

A DISSERTATION
Submitted to the Faculty of the School of Canon Law of the Catholic University of America in Partial Fulfillment of the Requirements for the Degree of Doctor of Canon Law

THE CATHOLIC UNIVERSITY OF AMERICA PRESS
WASHINGTON, D. C.
1947

Nihil Obstat:

EDUARDUS G. ROELKER, S.T.D., J.C.D.,
Censor Deputatus.

Washingtonii, die 21 martii 1947.

Imprimatur:

✠D. CARD. DOUGHERTY,
Archiepiscopus Philadelphiensis.

Philadelphia, die 25 martii 1947.

To

My Mother

and

My Father

Table of Contents

PART TWO
The Methods Used for the Promulgation of Laws

Foreword

A necessary element in the institution of any law is the element of its promulgation. It is the purpose of this treatise to explain first of all the notion of promulgation, and secondly the methods used to promulgate the laws of the Church.

It is important to note that, although the present work is entitled *The Promulgation of Law,* in this treatment only the law of the Church has been considered. While it is true that the general remarks concerning the nature of promulgation and its necessity are applicable to all law, still the civil law has not been considered except for the Roman Law, and this has been included only because of its close connection with the Canon Law.

As far as any commentary on the canons of the Code of Canon Law is concerned, there is presented in this work very little in the form of an explicit commentary on the canons. The subject of the promulgation of law did not lend itself to that type of canonical treatment, primarily because most of the law of the Code that deals with the promulgation of law is not new law. As a result an explanation of the meaning of the laws of the Code dealing with promulgation will be found in various parts of this work.

The present work is divided into two parts. The subject matter is divided and treated under the two general headings of the theory of promulgation and of the methods used to promulgate the laws of the Church. The various questions that require treatment as also the laws of the canons of the Code which concern the promulgation of Church law are discussed in the one or the other of the two parts of this work where it seemed most logical to treat them.

The first part, entitled *Theory of the Promulgation of Law,* is divided into two chapters. In the first chapter there is discussed the notion of promulgation. There is included in this chapter a study of the definition of promulgation and of the nature of the promulgation of law. The second chapter is concerned with the necessity of the element of promulgation. In this chapter is given an account of the controversy concerning the degree of the necessity of the promulgation of a law.

The second part, entitled *The Methods Used for the Promulgation of Laws,* consists of eight chapters. In them is presented a study of the various methods which have been used during the centuries of the Church's history for the promulgating of ecclesiastical laws. The first six chapters of this part deal with the methods used to promulgate universal pontifical legislation. In these six chapters two articles are devoted to the Roman Law, since it had a certain influence on the history of the promulgation of the laws of the Church, at least inasmuch as the opinion of some authors was influenced by the Roman Law. The seventh and eighth chapters of this second part treat of the promulgation of conciliar and episcopal laws of the Church.

The writer wishes to express his sincere gratitude to His Eminence, Dennis Cardinal Dougherty, Archbishop of Philadelphia, for the opportunity of advanced study in Canon Law; to the members of the faculty of the School of Canon Law for their scholarly direction and valuable assistance; and to all others who by their aid contributed towards the completion of this dissertation.

PART ONE

Theory of the Promulgation of Law

CHAPTER I

Notion of the Promulgation of Law

ARTICLE 1

Definition

In the best known definitions of law one finds mention of the promulgation of law. Saint Thomas Aquinas (1225-1274) in defining law called it a "regulation in accordance with reason promulgated by the head of the community for the sake of the common welfare."[1] And Suarez (1548-1617) described law as a "general precept, which is just and stable in its character and has been promulgated in a sufficient manner."[2] A law is, therefore, an expression of the will of the legislator, but since it is meant to be a norm governing the human actions of the community subject to the lawmaker, it must be officially proposed to this community as a binding rule of action. So there is included in the definition of law the element of its official notification, which is known as the promulgation of the law.

Etymologically the word promulgation comes from the Latin *pro-mulcare*, or more correctly from *pro-vulgare*, which means to place before the people, to announce to the public. Sextus Pompeius Festus (2nd cent. A.D.) in explaining this derivation declared that laws were said to be promulgated when for the first time they were put before the public *(vulgus)*.[3]

However, to fulfill the notion of promulgation in its juridic nature more is necessary than the mere publication of the law.

1 "Quaedam rationis ordinatio ad bonum commune, et ab eo qui curam communitatis habet, promulgata."—*Summa Theologica*, I.II., q. 90, a. 4, in corp. Cf. Cicognani, *Canon Law* (authorized English version by O'Hara and Brennan, 2.ed., Philadelphia: Dolphin Press, 1935), p. 523.

2 "Lex est commune praeceptum, justum ac stabile, sufficienter promulgatum."—*De Legibus et Legislatore Deo*, Lib. I, c. xii, n. 4 (hereafter cited as *De Legibus*)—*Opera Omnia* (28 vols., ed. Vivés, Parisiis, 1856-1861), Vols. V-VI, *De Legibus et Legislatore Deo*.

3 Mueller, *Sexti Pompeii Festi de Verborum Significatione quae supersunt* (Lipsiae, 1839), p. 224.

A law is said to be promulgated when it is publicly proposed to the community by the lawmaker himself or on his authority, so that the will of the legislator to impose an obligation can become known to his subjects. So Wernz-Vidal define promulgation as "the announcement of a law made to the community on the authority of the head of the community."[4] The definition of Vermeersch-Creusen is equally good: "The promulgation of a law is the solemn announcement of the law, so that it can become known to the community."[5]

From a study of these two definitions and those given by other authors it is clear that there are two elements necessary in order that the notion of promulgation be realized. First, the intimation or announcement of the law must be public. It must be an external manifestation of the law to the community as such. It is not sufficient that this announcement of the law be made privately to the individual members of the community, even if, perhaps, all the subjects were reached. Inherently a law pertains to the community. Since the obligation of a law is imposed directly on the community, and on individuals only inasmuch as they are members of the community, the law must be publicly presented to the community as such. Secondly, the announcement of the law must be authentic. It must be made on the authority of the lawgiver, i. e., either by the lawmaker himself or by one legitimately delegated to act in his name, so that it is constituted as an official announcement. It is this element which lacks mention in the definition of Sextus Pompeius Festus, and so his definition is useful only etymologically inasmuch as it shows the derivation of the word *promulgare*.

In general, it can be said that for the institution of a law there is necessary a promulgation which is made by means of an external apprehensible proposition of the law, whereby it becomes morally possible for the law to come to the notice of the whole community. It is not necessary that all the subjects

---

[4] "Promulgatio est legis publicatio communitati facta auctoritate illius qui curam habet communitatis."—*Ius Canonicum* (7 vols. in 8, Romae: Apud Aedes Universitatis Gregorianae, 1923-1938. Vol. I, 1938), I, 186.

[5] "Legis sollemnis intimatio, ita ut communitati innotescere possit."—*Epitome Iuris Canonici* (2.ed., 3 vols., Mechliniae-Romae: Dessain, 1924-1925), I, 52.

actually know about the law. Consequently the lawmaker does not have to make known his law by means of a special mandate or letter to each individual whom he intends to bind by the law.[6] It would be morally impossible to find a method of promulgation which would insure that a knowledge of the law would come to each and every subject, for many even slight and accidental causes could prevent a number of subjects from actually obtaining a knowledge of the law.[7] But it is necessary that the head of the community present his law to the community in such a way that it becomes morally possible for the subjects to obtain knowledge of the law. Finally, there is no fixed and invariable time limit within which the law must come to the notice of every subject of the lawmaker in order that the law be considered as promulgated.

In the process of the enacting of a law various moments or successive stages can be distinguished. Which of these when realized produces the real efficacy of promulgation? V. del Giudice holds that since the state recognizes two stages in the promulgation of a law—the first an act by which the law is drawn up by a competent authority, and the second an act by which the existence of the new legislative precept is publicly announced to the citizens so that they may learn of the law—this same distinction should be applied to ecclesiastical laws.[8] But only the second of these acts can be called promulgation in the strict sense of the term. It would be more correct to say instead that there are two stages in the process of the instituting of a law, the one that of the law's emanation from the legitimate authority, and the other that of the law's promulgation by the same authority. It can be seen clearly from the canons of the Code[9] that only the second of these produces a juridic effect, for in canon 8 it is stated that laws are instituted when they are promulgated, and in canon 9 there is mentioned the approved method whereby the laws of the Holy See become promulgated.

---

6 C. 1, X, *de postulatione praelatorum*, I, 5.

7 Cf. Suarez, *De Legibus*, Lib. III, c. xvi, n. 4.

8 Quoted by Gillet, "De lege data et nondum promulgata,"—*Jus Pontificium*, VIII (1928), 216.

9 Canon 8, §1, and canon 9.

This consists in the publication of the law in the official organ of the Holy See.[10]

The opinion of del Giudice is not admissible in consequence of the conclusion he draws. He distinguishes, as was mentioned above, two acts or moments in the promulgation of a law, the one the emanation of the law from a competent authority, and the second the publication of the law. But he claims that each of these acts produces its own juridic effect. He argues that the two acts are certainly distinct, and that they may even be separated by a relatively long period of time. The day of the drawing up of the prescription of a law almost never coincides with the day on which it is published. For example, the Code itself was issued on May 27, 1917, but it was not published in the *Acta Apostolicae Sedis* until June 28 of the same year. If this is true, then what is the juridic condition of the prescription of a law which has indeed been drawn up, but which has not been promulgated? Del Giudice says that a law not yet promulgated does have some juridic effect; that it does produce an obligation, since it binds the officials of the Curia, whose duty it is to see to the promulgation of the law.

This theory cannot be sustained in the light of canon 8, §1, of the Code of Canon Law. It is the common opinion of authors that the promulgation of the law is necessary for the binding power of the law, so that the law not yet promulgated has also no juridic effect. There is no such thing as a partial promulgation of the law. Authors differ only in their opinion concerning the measure or degree of this necessity. Accordingly, before the law is promulgated, it produces no juridic effect. The members of the Curia are not bound by it any more than anyone else is.

The members of the Curia are of course bound to see to the promulgation of the law, but this obligation arises from a source other than the law which is to be promulgated. Most probably the law is not even directed toward them. The obligation, therefore, arises from their office, the responsibilities of which are regulated by the law and the practice which obtains in the

---

[10] "Leges ab Apostolica Sede latae promulgantur per editionem in *Actorum Apostolicae Sedis commentario officiali,* nisi in casibus particularibus alius promulgandi modus fuerit praescriptus; . . ."

Curia. Gillet does not deny that there can be distinguished a number of moments or steps in the promulgation of a law, for he readily acknowledges that a series of acts can be evolved for the ultimate sufficient promulgation of a law. But it must always be conceded that it is at one definite moment that the law is finally to be considered as sufficiently promulgated, and it is at that moment that the law is instituted. One of these acts will actually produce the juridic effect of the institution of the law.

ARTICLE 2

Promulgation of Law is not the Same as the Enactment of the Law or Divulging of the Law or the Notice of the Law

From what has been said, then, it can be seen that the promulgation of a law is not the same as the enactment *(editio)*[11] of a law, whether undertaken privately by the law-maker or publicly in council. For even when a law is enacted publicly it is not considered promulgated until it has been officially presented to the community as binding.[12]

Promulgation differs, too, from the divulgation of a law. The latter denotes the act of bringing to the notice of the individual subjects a law which has already been promulgated. As Suarez has said, it is the application of the first promulgation to the notice of the absent subjects, inasmuch as these were not able to read or to hear the initial promulgation.[13]

Promulgation and divulgation differ first of all in their respective authors, for the author of promulgation must be the lawmaker or one who acts in his name by reason of an authentic delegation. On the other hand, the author of the divulgation of a law can be any person who spreads knowledge of the law. No official status is required in the author of the divulgation of a law, for the law

---

[11] In this article the term "enactment" is used as the closest English equivalent of the term "*editio*," which is the technical term used by authors for signifying the process whereby the text of the law is drawn up. It does not mean the same as the term "*editio*" as used in canon 9 of the Code.

[12] Suarez, *De Legibus*, Lib. III, c. xvi, n. 2.

[13] *De Legibus*, Lib. III, c. xvi, n. 3.

can be published by private persons in sermons, in articles, in periodicals, etc.

Again, the passive subject of promulgation is the community on which the law is imposed; the individual is not involved except in so far as he is a member of the community. Divulgation, on the other hand, has as its primary passive subject the individual member of the community.

Finally, these two concepts differ in their proper effect. Promulgation of the law effects the perfection of the law. It is when the law has been promulgated that it begins to be a true norm having the power to bind. As a result there arises from the act of promulgation an objective obligation; the law binds *in actu primo*. From the divulgation of the law there arises a knowledge of the law on the part of the individual subjects. This fact makes them conscious of the law, and consequently produces a subjective obligation; the law binds *in actu secundo*.

Notice of a law *(notitia)* is subjective knowledge of the law. This also differs from the notion of the promulgation of law. It is possible for the individual subjects to know of the law before it has been promulgated by the lawmaker, but this knowledge produces no obligation of itself. However, when a law is promulgated it is instituted, and hence it is *in actu primo* obligatory for all the subjects of the law. This means that the law of itself has a binding force as soon as it is promulgated, even though there may be individual subjects who do not yet know of the law. Notice of the promulgated law produces an obligation *in actu secundo*, a subjective obligation, since by knowledge the individual becomes bound by the law in the internal form. As a result, when upon its promulgation notice of the law is had, its transgression is morally imputable.

Acceptance of the new law by the subjects is not part of the promulgation of the law, nor does it constitute any juridical element in a law, for the law obtains its force from the will of the lawmaker independently of the consent of the people. If a law depended for its obligatory power on the consent of those who are to be bound by it, then the authority of the head of the community would be destroyed. It is true that Gratian says:

"Leges instituuntur cum promulgantur, firmantur cum moribus utentium comprobantur."[14] However, this is no indication that the consent of the public is necessary for the instituting of a law. It is one thing to institute a law, but quite another to make it firm. Gratian spoke not of any intrinstic firmness which the law did not have previously, but only of an external and accidental stability. Laws are indeed made firm *de facto* by the practice and the usage of the people, but *de iure* laws do not thus acquire any added juridical import, since they are firmly established *de iure* by their legitimate institution. Hence the acceptance of a law by the people is not to be identified with the promulgation of the law which they receive.

Finally, it should be noted here that the use of the term promulgation is not a precise one when applied with reference to the pronouncement of a penal sentence. Sentences, since they are not laws, do not need promulgation in the sense in which the term is understood in this dissertation, for the reason that a sentence need be made known only to the individuals who are affected by it. Probably the reason that the term promulgation was applied to the publication of sentences was that sentences were at one time very often made known to the parties concerned in the same way as laws were made known, namely, by the placing of a copy of the text of the sentence in a public place.

Article 3

The Time when a Law Begins to Bind

It is important in the determination of the time when a law begins to bind to have a clear understanding of the meaning and kinds of obligation. The obligation that results from a law is active and passive. The former obligation is that which is formally in the law itself; it is the law's power of binding. A passive obligation exists in the subject, and it means his duty to obey.

An active obligation gives rise to a passive obligation in those subject to the law. The passive obligation that results from the active obligation is a merely material, i. e., purely objective obligation, if it really exists, but because of a lack of knowledge is not

[14] C. 3, D. IV.

adverted to by the subject. This is the objective subordination which results from the application of the law to the subjects by means of the promulgation of the law. The obligation becomes formal and subjective when the subject obtains knowledge of the objective obligation which was imposed by the law as soon as it had been instituted. It is to be noted that the active and merely material passive obligations exist independently of the knowledge of the subject; they depend solely on the institution of the law.

When mention is made of an obligation *in actu primo* in this work, the merely material passive obligation is meant. The term *in actu secundo* refers to the formal passive obligation. It is true that all authors do not use these two terms *in actu primo* and *in actu secundo* with the same meaning that is attached to them here. But there is no uniform meaning given to these two terms by the authors, so that the meaning attached to the two terms by one author may be entirely different from that given to them by another.

In the history of canon law there has been among authors a difference of opinion as to the exact time when a law begins to bind. The first statement in ecclesiastical law concerning the element of promulgation in relation to the concept of law was that of Gratian, who in his *dictum* on a text of Saint Augustine (354-430)[15] advanced the principle which has now become incorporated in the Code of Canon Law as canon 8, §1: "Leges instituuntur cum promulgantur."[16] It may well be noted here that, since the present Code of Canon Law merely restates the law as it was before the Code,[17] the norm of canon 6, 2°, of the Code becomes applicable,[18] so that the interpretations of the approved pre-Code authors are to be accepted as illustrative also of the present law.

By saying that laws are instituted when they are promulgated Gratian indicated that promulgation is the final step in the process of the making of a law. With its promulgation a law becomes en-

[15] *De Vera Religione*, c. 31—Migne, *Patrologiae Cursus Complctus, Series Latina* (221 vols., Parisiis, 1844-1864), XXXIV, 147 (hereafter cited as *MPL*).

[16] *Dicta* p. c. 3, D. IV.

[17] Canon 8, §1.

[18] "Canones qui ius vetus ex integro referunt, ex veteris iuris auctoritate, atque ideo ex receptis apud probatos auctores interpretationibus, sunt aestimandi."

dowed with all the qualities necessary to make it binding. In other words, by promulgation the law is perfected and completed, so that it begins for the first time to exist as a norm of action which is binding on the community. Michiels calls the day of the promulgation of a law the birthday of the law.[19]

Even though it is true that laws are instituted when they are promulgated, so that according to Gratian and the present Code the institution of the law occurs simultaneously with its promulgation, the two terms are not synonymous. The Code does not mean to identify these two notions, for clearly they are not the same. A law is said to be instituted when it becomes endowed with all the qualities which are necessary to satisfy the notion of law, that is, to make it a binding rule of conduct for the subjects of the lawmaker. One may say that promulgation is a step—always the final one—in the institution of a law.

It is presupposed that all the necessary preliminary stages have been evolved before the law is finally promulgated. If the two notions of promulgation and institution were identical, then it would be true that every time a law or an ordinance has been promulgated it would at the same time be instituted. But this is not necessarily so, since it is possible for an ordinance to be promulgated and yet not to be instituted as a law, inasmuch as there is lacking some quality necessary for the essence of a law, e. g., if something were commanded which it is not morally possible for the subjects to obey. Therefore the *dictum* of Gratian as quoted in canon 8 indicates simply at what moment a law can truly be called a law. It does not demonstrate that the institution and the promulgation of a law are identical notions.

According to the Code, therefore, a law begins to bind only when it has been solemnly published by the authority of the legislator in such a way that it is possible for the subject community to know of the law. But precisely at what moment does a law of its own nature begin to bind? Among authors before the twentieth century there was a sharp difference of opinion concerning the time when an ecclesiastical law began to bind. The controversy itself was occasioned by a difference of opinion, not

[19] *Normae Generales Juris Canonici* (2 vols., Lublin: Universitas Catholica, 1929), I, 153.

concerning the promulgation of the law, but rather regarding the period of time during which the enacted and published ecclesiastical law continued as yet inoperative in its binding effect *(vacatio legis)*. In view of this a discussion of that controversy has no direct pertinence in the present work.

On the other hand, inasmuch as two of the three defended opinions directly do concern the promulgation of law, and inasmuch as both of these opinions are still defended as regards the time when a law of its very nature *(ex natura sua)* begins to bind, they will be examined more closely. The third opinion was that of a number of authors who held that the inoperative period of two months, as provided for in civil law of Justinian (527-565),[20] was to be extended to ecclesiastical law, so that no general ecclesiastical laws began to bind *in actu secundo* until two months after their promulgation, unless the lawmaker expressly provided otherwise. This opinion has, of course, become obsolete, since the law of the Code has provided for *vacatio legis* of three months from the time of the promulgation for all laws of the Holy See.[21]

Many authors held in the past, and at present most of those who mention the question at all seem likewise to hold, that as soon as a law has been publicly promulgated in a suitable place it begins to bind in the whole territory for which it was made according to the power and the jurisdiction of the legislator. The lawmaker may expressly state that the law does not bind until a certain date, and he does this when he provides a period after the promulgation during which the subjects are not bound *in actu secundo* to obey the law. Some of the authors, including mostly the older moralists and the commentators of the doctrine of Saint Thomas, taught explicitly that a law begins to bind as soon as it has been promulgated. [22]

---

[20] N. 66.

[21] Canon 9.

[22] Bonacina, *Opera Omnia* (ed. postrema, 3 vols., Venetiis, 1687), II, Tr. XII, disp. 1, q. 1, punc. 4, n. 17; Bouquillon, *Theologia Moralis Fundamentalis* (2.ed., Brugis, 1890), p. 275; Gury, *Compendium Theologiae Moralis* (2.ed., 2 vols., Romae, 1869), I, 77; Navarrus, *Opera Omnia* (6 vols., Venetiis, 1618), V, consil. I, *de constitutionibus*, n. 15; Panormitanus (Nicholaus de Tudeschis), *Commentaria in Quinque Libros Decretalium* (5 vols. in 7, Venetiis, 1588), in c. 2, X, *de constutionibus*, I, 2, n. 7; Pirhing, *Jus Canonicum in V Libros Decretalium* (ed. novissima, 4 vols., Dilingae, 1722), Lib. I, tit. I, sec. I, §4, n. 30; Vasquez, *Commentariorum ac Disputationum in Primam Secundae Sancti Thomae Tomus Secundus* (ed. novissima, 2 vols., Lugduni, 1631), disp. 156, c. 3, n. 14.

Among the moderns there are very few who even mention this problem. The reason for this seems to be that they take it for granted as being understood from the words of the Code that a law binds as soon as it has been promulgated. Chelodi (1880-1922) expressly stated that laws bind as soon as they have been promulgated.[23] But even though it is not mentioned explicitly by many authors that the law has its binding power immediately upon its promulgation, it can be deduced from what they say about the nature of promulgation that they consider a law to be binding as soon as it has been promulgated. Modern authors are unanimous in maintaining that a law is perfectly constituted as soon as it has been promulgated. Furthermore, they agree that promulgation need be made only in such a way that it becomes morally possible for the law to come to the notice of the community. This theory is supported by the words of the Code, since the Code states clearly that laws are instituted when they are promulgated,[24] and it then immediately indicates the method of promulgation for laws enacted by the Holy See. Accordingly, as soon as that method has reached its actual fulfillment, the law binds of its very nature, since it is then that it is instituted. The lapse of time produces no effect except that the laws come to the notice of more subjects. Since it is not necessary for the law to be known in order that it bind *in actu primo,* no lapse of time after its promulgation is inherently required before the law begins to bind itself.

Other words of the Code support this theory. In canon 9 the Code states of laws of the Holy See: ". . . vim suam exerunt tantum expletis tribus mensibus a die qui *Actorum* numero appositus est, . . ."[25] It is the use of the word *exserere* which is significant. It means to thrust, to project, hence to reveal, or to disclose. The idea expressed by this phrase as used in canon 9 is not that the law has its power for the first time at the end of the three-month period, but rather that then for the first time it discloses or reveals the power which it already has.

Another argument can be drawn from the text of canon 9 to

[23] *Ius Canonicum de Personis* (3.ed. curavit Pius Ciprotti, Vicenza: Societá Anonima Tipografica, 1942), p. 102.
[24] Canon 8, §1.
[25] Canon 9.

show that the binding force of the law does not depend on any lapse of time after promulgation of the law. The final words of canon 9 show that the legislator considers the method of promulgation prescribed in this canon to be sufficient of itself to institute laws of the Holy See. For it is indicated in the canon that some laws by their very nature do not admit of a *vacatio legis* and that in other cases the lawmaker is free to dispense with the three-month period as he sees fit.

The words of St. Thomas support this theory, for he held that those for whom the law had been promulgated were bound to observe the law in so far as it actually came to their notice, or could come to their notice through others, once the promulgation had been made. In other words, as long as it was possible for the law to become known from the promulgation, that promulgation was considered sufficient to effect the institution of the law.

Suarez, however, though he admitted that many authors did hold this opinion, nevertheless declared that to him it had always seemed difficult to support this doctrine.[26] The reason he gave for this was that it exceeded the power of the head of the community to bind all his subjects by a law as soon as he had solemnly published the new law in only one place. The ruler could not do this, so Suarez maintained, even though he wanted to do it. In support of his contention Suarez advanced several arguments.

First of all, notice of the law among the community was necessary if the law actually was to become obligatory. Therefore, in order that the law could become obligatory it was at least necessary that it be possible for the law to come to the notice of the subjects. But it was not true that, when the promulgation was made only in one place, the law could become immediately known to all the subjects in the whole territory. So it was impossible for the law to become binding before there had elapsed a period of time which proved sufficient to let the notice of the law gain currency in the whole territory.

Secondly, if the law was proposed privately or quietly in the royal palace, it could not have the power to oblige the community, since it had not been proposed in such a way as to be accomodated

[26] *De Legibus,* Lib. III, c. xvii, n. 3.

to the potential cognizance of the community. Similarly, although it was promulgated in one place, that was not sufficient to let the law become obligatory upon the whole kingdom immediately.

Finally, Suarez argued that this teaching was confirmed by Saint Thomas, who stated that the law obliged only inasmuch as its promulgation by itself or through others could come to the knowledge of all.

From the discussion as thus far reported it could appear that Suarez held that a law does not bind, even when it has been solemnly promulgated, until such a time that the law can come to the notice of *all* the subjects of the lawmaker. But in his next paragraph[27] he showed that this was not what he meant, for his first conclusion was exactly the same as that of the first opinion, which the larger number of authors held, namely, that as soon as a law was sufficiently promulgated in the proper place, then without any lapse of time it began to bind immediately of its very nature.

It is from his second conclusion that it becomes apparent where the difference lay between Suarez and the majority of the authors. It was not so much a difference concerning whether or not the law bound as soon as it had been promulgated, as it might first seem. Rather, being perfectly agreed that every law bound as soon as it had been sufficiently promulgated, they disagreed as to when the law was to be considered sufficiently promulgated. It was the conclusion of Suarez that, although a law may have been sufficiently promulgated in one place and thus may have begun to bind there, it did not follow that the law by that first act of promulgation was immediately also promulgated in a sufficient way in the rest of the territory, which was, perhaps, quite a distance from the place of the first promulgation. So it could require some additional time before the law could be brought to the notice of the persons who lived some distance away, and before it could be considered sufficiently promulgated in these places. This stand was to be maintained even though the law-maker had definitely stated that the law was sufficiently promulgated by means of the first promulgation. Suarez showed that it

27 *De Legibus*, Lib. III, c. xvii, n. 5.

was the question of the sufficiency of the promulgation with which he was concerned when he stated that he did not see how it was possible for men living in remote regions to be bound by a law when they were invincibly ignorant of the law, since it was impossible for them to know of the law from the promulgation made only in a distant place.[28]

In answer to the arguments which Suarez advanced, it can well be admitted that, for a law to become binding *in actu secundo,* notice of it is necessary, and for a law to become binding *in actu primo,* the law must be promulgated in such a way that it is possible for the law to come to the notice of the subjects. But simply in view of the fact that not all the subjects have gained an immediate knowledge of the law when it was promulgated in a given place, it does not follow that the law is not sufficiently promulgated, or that it does not bind even *in actu primo.* For a law is considered sufficiently promulgated not only when all the subjects have become aware of the law. Rather, when the law is presented to the community in such a way that it is morally possible for the community to know of the law, then it is instituted as a law and is binding at least objectively. Once the law has been publicly proclaimed in one part of the territory of the lawmaker, it can be considered as sufficiently promulgated, provided only that it is possible for the entire community subject to the legislator to know of the law.

From the law of the Code[29] it is clear that after the promulgation nothing more is needed to complete the instituting of the law. Any divulgation of the promulgated law is superfluous as far as the law itself in its native binding force is concerned. Suarez himself admitted that once a law was sufficiently promulgated, i. e., as soon as the space of time necessary that the law be able to come to the notice of those who lived in remote regions had elapsed, the law bound in the whole territory. He stated further that all in the territory were bound, even if for some reason the notice of the law had not come within the cognizance of a certain number of the people, or even when it had not spread to a certain part of the territory.[30] Now, if this held true when some period of

[28] *De Legibus,* Lib. III, c. xvii, n. 7.

[29] Canon 8, §1.

[30] *De Legibus,* Lib. III, c. xvii, n. 11.

time had elapsed, it should also hold true immediately from the first promulgation of the law, provided only that the act of promulgation sufficed to establish the possibility for all the subjects to obtain a knowledge of the law. Bouquillon (1840-1902) expressed this very idea when he declared that the act of promulgation in one place sufficed to attach a binding force to the law even if a knowledge of the law was acquired only later in the remoter parts of the world.[31]

The answer given to the first argument of Suarez above is equally valid with reference to his second argument. It is quite possible that by an act of promulgation in one place a law becomes sufficiently public that it can become known to all the subjects, even those at a distance. It matters not that this may take some time, for the length of time it takes to obtain knowledge of the law does not affect the validity of the promulgation. It is not necessary that the law actually come to the notice of the whole community at one time immediately upon its promulgation; it suffices for an adequate promulgation that the law *can* come to the notice of all at least mediately and successively.[32] It must, of course, always be granted that the promulgated law which binds the subjects *in actu primo* does not at the same bind them *in actu secundo* as long as they are inculpably ignorant of the law.

Finally, it can be noted that the words of Saint Thomas seem rather to be an argument against what was held by Suarez, for Saint Thomas stated very clearly, "in so far as its (the law's) promulgation *can* come to the notice of all either of itself or through others."[33] He did not state that the promulgated law must actually have come to the notice of all; he simply declared that it must be possible for the law to come to the notice of all.

In reference to the second conclusion of Suarez[34] it is noted that Suarez declared that the law began to bind in the various parts of the territory at different times. But it is to be remembered that as soon as a law is sufficiently promulgated it is instituted

[31] *Theologia Moralis Fundamentalis*, p. 271.

[32] Vecchiotti, *Institutiones Canonicae ex operibus Joannis Card. Soglia excerptae* (16.ed., 3 vols., Augustae Taurinorum, 1875), I, 31.

[33] *Summa Theologica*, I.II., q. 90, a. 4, ad 2um. Italics supplied by the writer.

[34] *De Legibus*, Lib. III, c. xvii, n. 6.

and it begins to be binding not only for some but for all the subjects of the lawmaker.

Finally, Suarez spoke of the duration of time during which the law was not binding as a matter that was to be decided "*pro prudenti arbitrio.*"[35] But he did not state who was to make this prudent judgment, and in consequence there would be a difference of opinion as to what the exact duration of time would be for a certain place. Thus a law could be evaded by those who actually did know of the law, but who claimed that it did not yet bind them, since it was not yet to be considered sufficiently promulgated in their territory. If anyone could decide whether or not a method of promulgation be sufficient to make it morally possible for the law to come to the notice of all the subjects, surely such a decision is most competently made by the lawmaker, especially if the lawmaker is the Church. And if the lawmaker declares that the law binds all his subjects as soon as it has first been promulgated, then there should be no further question concerning the matter. Even if he does not expressly state that the law binds immediately *in actu secundo* for those who know of the law, still that is to be understood unless he expressly allows a period of time during which the subjects who do know of the law are obliged to comply with the provisions of the law. Vermeersch-Creusen remark that a human legislator will act prudently if he holds to the custom of granting a deferment of the obligation of his laws until he is morally certain that they have become known to the community.[36]

In consideration of the words of canons 8, §1 and 9, the only conclusion that can be drawn concerning the time when a promulgated law of its nature begins to bind is that it binds the entire community *in actu primo* as soon as it is sufficiently promulgated. To say, as Suarez did, that it may require some time to accomplish a sufficient promulgation of the law in all parts of the territory, and that as a result the law binds in one place before it binds in another part of the territory, does not seem consonant with the theory of promulgation. For it seems that the act by which a law is promulgated should be of itself sufficient to make it possible

---

35 *De Legibus*, Lib. III, c. xvii, n. 6.
36 *Epitome Iuris Canonici*, I, 53.

for the entire community to come to the knowledge of the law. If this is true, then the law binds; no additional lapse of time is demanded. If it should happen that someone was inculpably ignorant of the law, he would, of course, not be held accountable for his material violation of the law, nor would his act be punishable as a formal transgression of the law. A material offense against a law which binds objectively *(in actu primo)* can never become the equivalent of a formal violation of a law, which postulates that the law binds also subjectively *(in actu secundo).*

Article 4

The Condition of a Law That has been Promulgated but has not yet Become Operative because of a Vacatio Legis

There arises another question which is related to that which concerns the time when a law of its nature begins to bind. That question is the following: What is the condition of a law which has been promulgated, but which has not begun to be binding subjectively because of a period of time provided by the lawmaker during which the subjects are not bound to obey the law *(vacatio legis)*? Since this happens now in the case of all laws of the Holy See as long as no different provision is specifically indicated, the question could be phrased, thus: What is the condition of a law of the Holy See after it has been published in the *Acta Apostolicae Sedis,* but before the three-month period designated in canon 9 has elapsed?

Suarez taught that a law has no binding power until the end of the *vacatio legis* in view of the very condition of the law itself which until then is not as yet perfectly constituted. His reason for this doctrine was that before the end of the period of time allotted for its divulgation a law was not to be considered as sufficiently promulgated or manifested.[37] He declared this doctrine to be confirmed by the fact that during the period of the *vacatio legis* even those who know about it are not bound.

First of all, it is to be noted that elsewhere Suarez admits that obligation is the adequate effect of law. Every law must give rise

[37] *De Legibus,* Lib. III, c. xviii, n. 5.

to an obligation of some sort. He asserts that it is not possible to have a law which does not impose an obligation on the community, and that this is the common opinion of theologians.[38] Therefore Suarez did not assert that a law sufficiently promulgated had no binding power when the legislator granted a *vacatio legis.* He said that the law was not instituted until after the period of grace granted by the lawmaker because until then the law was not yet sufficiently promulgated.

From what has been said in the previous article it is clear that a law can and does bind immediately upon its promulgation. Hence it depends entirely on the will of the lawmaker whether a *vacatio legis* will be granted, for at no time is it demanded by the nature of law. It is by means of the promulgation of the law that the law is instituted. By that is meant that the law becomes perfect, complete and endowed with all the qualities necessary to make it an obligatory norm of action. From the words of the Code there can no longer be any doubt as to when promulgation takes place, for the law states clearly: "Leges ab Apostolica Sede latæ promulgantur per editionem in *Actorum Apostolicæ Sedis commentario officiali. . . .* " When, therefore, a law appears in a copy of the *Acta,* the law is to be considered promulgated. Any opinion, then, which would contend that the promulgation of the law is not complete until the lapse of the *vacatio legis* would not be in harmony with the canons of the Code.[39] In the previous article it was shown from the text of the canons of the Code that a law begins to bind as soon as it is promulgated, even before the end of the *vacatio legis.* Furthermore, there is nothing in the Code that indicates that during the period of the *vacatio legis* the law has no binding power.

The solution to the problem seems to lie in the distinction between the various kinds of obligations imposed by a law. It is certainly possible for law to produce an objective (merely material passive) obligation in an individual subject. And there seems to be no reason for denying that the law can still have its objective force even when it does not have a subjective application for any subject. The nature of a law does not demand

[38] *De Legibus,* Lib. I, c. xiv, nn. 4, 12.
[39] Canons 8, §1; 9.

that it impose a subjective obligation *(in actu secundo)*, but merely that it impose an obligation on the community to which it is directed, for the community is the object of law. This obligation on the community as such produces an obligation *in actu primo* in the subjects even though they may not be bound *in actu secundo*. For example, it is possible that a law be directed at a class of persons in the Church, and these persons at present have no existence. Then the law does not automatically cease to exist or lose its binding power, as can be seen from the fact that it will impose an obligation on any person of that class who begins to exist at a later date. The law in that case needs no reinstitution, no new promulgation, and this is evidence that the law still had its binding power even when no subjects were bound by it.

It is quite possible, too, that by means of a dispensation all those who are actually bound *in actu secundo* by a law be excused from the observance of the law, so that actually no one person is bound to follow the law. The law does not cease to exist, and it needs no new promulgation when the dispensation is no longer effective. The law exists and so produces an obligation even when all the subjects are actually excused from the formal obligation.

The condition of a newly promulgated law which is instituted, but does not yet impose any obligation *in actu secundo* because of a *vacatio legis*, is similar to the condition of the law in the two cases given above. It must be admitted that laws are instituted as soon as they are sufficiently promulgated. Furthermore, laws of the Holy See are promulgated by the publication in the *Acta Apostolicæ Sedis*.[40] Therefore, as soon as laws of the Holy See are published in the *Acta*, they are instituted as true laws, and they must produce an obligation. It is clear that ordinarily no subjective obligation exists in any subject to obey these laws until the end of the three-month period. The obligation produced by the law before the end of the three-month period must be a merely material passive obligation *(in actu primo)*. The purpose of the *vacatio legis* then, is to defer the formal passive

---

[40] Canons 8, §1; 9.

obligation of the law until a time when notice of the law will have reached most of the subjects.

This is evidently what Sipos means when, while he defines the *vacatio legis* as the interval of time between the promulgation of the law and the beginning of its obligation, he states that a promulgated law immediately has force *(valet)*, but that the obligation does not arise until the end of the period of freedom allowed by the superior.[41] This point is well explained by Rodrigo. He teaches that after its promulgation the law applies to the community with its proper efficacy which it derives from the moment of its promulgation. The established *vacatio legis* produces this effect, that the beginning of the effective urgency of the law is deferred to some time after the promulgation of the law.[42]

In answer to the argument of Suarez one can, of course, fully admit that, even on those who know of it the law does not impose an obligation *in actu secundo* until after the period of grace has ended. But that implies simply the absence of a subjective obligation. It is possible for the law to bind *in actu primo,* i. e., objectively, without at the same time binding *in actu secundo,* i. e., subjectively.

It is the unanimous opinion of authors both old and recent that a law which is only doubtfully promulgated does not bind.[43]. The sole reason given is that a doubtful law does not bind, for as long as a law is not certainly promulgated it is to be treated as a doubtful law. The liberty possessed by the subjects cannot be restricted except by means of a certainly promulgated law. Marc (1831-1887) taught, however, that a doubtfully promulgated law was binding once it had been accepted by common usage.[44]

---

[41] *Enchiridion Iuris Canonici* (Pécs: Ex Typographia "Haladás R. T.," 1926), p. 19.

[42] *Praelectiones Theologico-Morales Comillenses,* Tomus II, *Tractatus De Legibus* (Santander: Sal Terrae, 1944), p. 152 (hereafter cited as *De Legibus*).

[43] St. Alphonsus Maria de Liguori, *Theologia Moralis* (ed. nova cura et studio P. Leonardi Gaudé, 4 vols., Romae, 1905-1912), Lib. I, n. 97; Gury, *Compendium Theologiae Moralis,* I, 78; Marc, *Institutiones Morales Alphonsianae* (2 vols., Romae, 1885), I, 104; Merkelbach, *Summa Theologiae Moralis ad Mentem D. Thomae et ad Normam Iuris Novi* (3.ed., 3 vols., Parisiis: Desclée, 1938), I, 212 (hereafter cited as *Summa Theologiae Moralis*); Salmanticenses, *Cursus Theologiae Moralis* (4 vols. Venetiis, 1714-1715), Tr. XI, *de legibus,* c. 2, n. 110.

[44] *Institutiones Morales Alphonsianae,* I, 104.

Chapter II

The Necessity of Promulgation

Article 1

Promulgation of a Law is Necessary

It is quite clear from a study of the notion of promulgation—and hence it is the common opinion among the authors—that, if a law is to bind the subjects of the lawmaker, the law must be promulgated. The reasons given for the necessity of promulgation are as follows:

1. A law pertains directly to the community as a binding rule of action, for it is not immediately directed to individuals. If, then, the community is the object of this regulation, it is absolutely necessary that the existence of the regulation be made known to the community as such by means of an official publication made on the authority of the head of the community. A law is a sign of the will of the ruler by which he intends to influence and to bind the whole community. It is necessary, accordingly, that this sign be made public in such a way that the community is able to know the legislative will of the head of the community.
2. A law is a norm and a measure for the acts of the subjects, but this norm or rule cannot be efficacious unless it be possible for the subjects to recognize for certain that the rule emanating from the legitimate ruler is of an obligatory character. So it must be published to the community authentically, i. e., on the authority of the lawmaker himself.
3. Although canon 8, §1, does not settle the controversy concerning whether promulgation is an essential element of law or merely a condition absolutely necessary for the existence of the law, still it does establish without a doubt that the promulgation of a law is absolutely necessary if

the law is to achieve a binding force. For by stating that laws are instituted when they are promulgated the Code implies that by promulgation a law becomes endowed with all the qualities necessary to make it an effective norm of action, that without promulgation the law can not have any binding force.

4. The classic definitions of law include the notion of promulgation as an element, thus showing that an official publication is necessary at least for the existence of a law.[1]
5. A law is the precept of a ruler acting in his capacity as a public person. It follows that the law should be announced in a public way. This, however, is only accomplished when the law is promulgated. Therefore the promulgation is necessary to make it possible for the subjects to distinguish two eventualities, namely, when the lawmaker speaks as a private person, and when he proposes a law in his official capacity.

Suarez (1548-1617) stated that of all the authors whom he consulted only one, Giovanni di Selva (16th cent.) contended that a law bound even apart from its publication if the lawmaker so wished.[2] But Suarez seemed to think that Selva did not really imply that no promulgation at all was necessary, but that he merely contended that a publication of a particular kind, namely one undertaken for a long period of time, or made with a certain degree of solemnity, was not required. In that sense, of course, Selva's statement would have been fully warranted, for the lawmaker is completely free to determine what method of publication is to be used, inasmuch as a promulgation with specifically defined solemnities is not demanded by the nature either of promulgation itself or of the law.

Even after Gratian had formulated the principle which is now incorporated in the Code,[3] there were some authors who made statements that seemed to deny the absolute necessity of the element of promulgation in the institution of a law. This denial was

---

1 E.g., St. Thomas Aquinas, *Summa Theologica*, I.II., q. 90, a. 4, in corp.; Suarez, *De Legibus*, Lib. I, c. xii, n. 4.

2 *De Legibus*, Lib. III, c. xvi, n. 1.

3 Compare the wording of c. 3, D. IV, in the Decree of Gratian and of canon 8, §1, in the Code.

occasioned by a text of Pope Innocent III (1198-1216), found in a letter written by the Pope to the dean and the chapter of the archdiocese of Sens. This letter was written in the year 1200. The occasion for it was the fact that a request had been made by the chapter of the archdiocese of Sens that the Pontiff allow Bishop Hugh of Auxerre, whom they had elected to their vacant see, to transfer from his diocese to the archdiocese of Sens.

The Pope answered with his letter "*Ad haec in B. Petro,*" refusing to grant permission because this same Hugh had failed to observe a papal interdict. The messenger of the chapter defended Bishop Hugh on the grounds that the papal interdict had not been made known to Hugh either by means of apostolic or personal letter, or by the Cardinal Legate or his representative, so that he was not bound to observe it. In his letter, however, the Pope answered that it was not necessary that the Bishop of Auxerre should have been informed personally of the interdict, since the Cardinal Legate had solemnly and publicly promulgated the interdict in the presence of many archbishops and bishops, and as a matter of fact many had observed it in France.[4]

Now, even though the case concerned the publication of a judicial sentence, the Pope in his answer did not confine himself to a consideration of judicial sentences, for he used the general term "constitution." As a result, his ruling applied to general papal legislation as well as to judicial sentences.

The words, *solemniter editam aut publice promulgatam,* were later on interpreted in various ways by the commentators of the Decretals. It was the word *aut* that caused the difficulty, since that word was generally regarded as having the force of a disjunctive particle; so the meaning implied in the phrase would have been that either a solemn enactment or a public promulgation was in itself sufficient for the instituting of a law, so that both were

---

[4] C. 1, X, *de postulatione praelatorum,* I, 5: "Nec sit necessarium, quum constitutio solemniter editur aut publice promulgatur, ipsius notitiam singulorum auribus per speciale mandatum vel literas inculcare; sed id solum sufficit, ut ad eius observantiam teneatur, qui noverit eam solemniter editam aut publice promulgatam; quum et contra quosdam, qui Sardicense concilium non servabant, tamquam illud non habuerint aut perceperint, canonica tradat auctoritas, quod eis non facile facultas credendi tribuitur, quum idem penes illos in suis regionibus actum fuerit et receptum."—Potthast, *Regesta Pontificium inde ab anno post Christum MCXCVIII ad MCCCIV* (2 vols., Berolini, 1874-1875), n. 1043; Augustinus, *Antiquae Decretalium Collectiones Commentariis et Emendationibus Illustratae* (Parisiis, 1621), F. 129.

not required together. It was in this way that some of the early commentators understood the text. In the thirteenth century Henricus de Segusio, better known as Hostiensis (†1271), taught that this passage was to be understood as meaning that, if the law was issued solemnly, then no public promulgation was necessary.[5] And Nicholaus de Tudeschis, known also as Abbas Panormitanus (1386-1453), in the fifteenth century likewise contended that from the use of the word *aut* in this text a good argument could be drawn in favor of the opinion that a constitution was binding even before it was solemnly or publicly promulgated, as long as it was issued in a solemn way.[6]

But from the doctrine of these two decretalists it is not to be inferred that in the centuries immediately following the promulgation of the Decretals of Gregory IX theirs was the only interpretation given to the text in question, for Friedberg (1837-1910) in his edition of the Decretals listed six early manuscripts which instead of the word *aut* use the copulative *ac.*[7] This is at least an indication that at that time also a public promulgation could have been considered necessary even for a law which had been issued solemnly.

Suarez (1548-1617) insisted that a public promulgation of the law to the community was absolutely essential to a law if it was to have binding force. He maintained that the word in question, *aut,* as used in the text of the letter of Pope Innocent III, was not disjunctive but copulative in its force, and for that reason was to be taken in the sense of *seu,* in which sense it often was used.[8] Accordingly, the two phrases *solemniter editam* and *publice promulgatam* were to be considered as equivalent in meaning, so that a law could not begin to bind unless it had been publicly promulgated. If by "solemnly enacted" was meant that the law was drawn up in a public council of the king or in the senate of a republic, that act alone did not suffice to institute the law; rather, the law also had to be presented to the community as a law before it bound them. Even conciliar law, which was most solemnly en-

[5] *In Primum Decretalium Librum Commentaria* (Venetiis, 1581), in c. 1, X, *de postulatione praelatorum,* I, 5, nn. 21, 22.

[6] *Omnia quae extant Commentaria* (Venetiis, 1588), in c. 1, X, *de postulatione praelatorum,* I, 5, n. 10.

[7] *Corpus Iuris Canonici,* II, col. 45, n. 28, to c. 1, X, *de postulatione praelatorum,* I, 5.

[8] *De Legibus,* Lib. III, c. xvi, n. 2.

acted, had to be promulgated. It was possible for the solemn enactment of the law and its promulgation to be accomplished through one and the same act. For example, if the solemn enactment of the law was made publicly before the assembled community for which the law was meant, then the solemn enactment of the law would have included the promulgation. When the two acts were distinct, then the solemn issuance was not sufficient to make the law binding apart from a public promulgation.[9]

After Suarez his teaching became the common teaching of the authors. It was held by Pirhing (1606-1679), who quoted Suarez to show that he agreed with his teaching,[10] by Pichler (1680-1736),[11] and by Schmalzgrueber (1663-1735). The latter taught that, even though it seemed from the use of *aut* in the text of decretal letter that with two things required disjunctively one would suffice, still a law had also to be publicly promulgated since the particle *aut* was really employed in that text as a conjunctive particle.[12] Finally, Saint Alphonsus Liguori (1696-1787), likewise agreeing with the interpretation of Suarez, stated that the two phrases, *solemniter editam* and *publice promulgatam*, represented merely two ways of saying the same thing,[13] and Zallinger (1735-1813) absolutely regarded the two phrases as implying an equivalent statement.[14]

Other authors, like Barbosa (1589-1649)[15] and those cited by him, inasmuch as they unconditionally held that a law did not bind until it had been solemnly and publicly promulgated, must have interpreted this text in the same way, even though they did not explicitly mention the text of the Decretals in their discussion.

Among the more recent authors, Bouix (1808-1870) was the only one who denied that an act of promulgation is necessary in consideration of the very nature of law. In support of what he held, he quoted a passage from Leurenius (1646-1723),[16] who declared

[9] Suarez, *De Legibus*, Lib. III, c. xvi, n. 2.

[10] *Jus Canonicum in V Libros Decretalium*, Lib. I, Tit. II, Sect. 1, §4, n. 26.

[11] *Candidatus Jurisprudentiae Sacrae* (4.ed., 5 vols., Augustae Vindelicorum, 1733), Lib. I, Tit. II, §2, n. 18.

[12] *Jus Ecclesiasticum Universum* (5 vols. in 12, Romae, 1843-1845), Lib. I, Tit. II, n. 26.

[13] *Theologia Moralis*, Lib. I, n. 96.

[14] *Institutiones Juris Ecclesiastici* (5 vols., Romae, 1823), I, 117.

[15] *Collectanea Doctorum tam veterum quam recentiorum in Jus Pontificium Universum* (6 vols., Lugduni, 1669), Lib. I, Tit. II, c. 2.

[16] *Jus Canonicum Universum* (5 vols. in 3, Venetiis, 1729), Lib. I, quaes. 40, n. 1.

that it could not be denied that a republic was able to grant to the legislator the power of binding his subjects by laws which had not been promulgated, and accordingly he admitted that it was possible for a law to exist with binding force even when it had not been promulgated. It is true that Leurenius did make this statement which Bouix attributed to him, but from that statement one can not rightfully conclude that Leurenius actually held the act of promulgation to be unnecessary for endowing the law with a binding force. On the contrary, he held that promulgation was an essential element of law.

Bouix himself had held in the first edition of his *Tractatus de Principiis Juris Canonici* that an act of promulgation was certainly required in order that any human law bind, and he stated that this was admitted by all. However, in his second edition of the same work he explained that in the tract *De Curia Romana,* Part III, Sec. 1, c. 2, he had reversed his stand. There he held that an act of promulgation is not necessary from the very nature of law, and that any eventual necessity for such an act would simply derive "*ex voluntate Principum,*" i.e., inasmuch as the lawmakers would not want their laws to become binding before a promulgation of them had been made.[17]

In commenting on this opinion, Michiels states that Bouix offers no serious argument against what is commonly held, and that Bouix himself admitted that ordinarily laws must be promulgated, since the omission of the act of promulgation could prove seriously detrimental to the welfare of the community.[18] The writer has found no author since the time of Bouix who holds that an act of promulgation is not necessary for a law in order that it be endowed with a binding force.

Article 2

The Degree of the Necessity of the Element of Promulgation

Agreeing, then, that to be binding a law must be promulgated, authors are confronted with the problem of the degree or measure of this necessity. Is promulgation so essential to the notion of law

[17] Cf. Bouix, *Tractatus de Principiis Juris Canonici* (2.ed., Parisiis), p. 231 (hereafter cited as *De Principiis*).

[18] Michiels, *Normae Generales Juris Canonici,* I, 152, ft. 4.

that it is an intrinsic and constituent element of law, or is it rather an element that is extrinsic, that is to say, a necessary condition or adjunct without which a law cannot exist? In essaying a solution of this problem, authors are far from agreement. Admittedly, in view of the fact that it makes no practical difference which opinion is held, the contention has become known among the authors as a "quæstio subtilior sed parum utilis."[19]

The history of this controversy indicates that in the fifteenth, sixteenth and seventeenth centuries the opinion that promulgation belongs to the essence of law was the more common opinion which was favored also by the more renowned authors of those times. During the last century, and especially among the post-Code authors, there has been a trend to the other opinion, namely, that promulgation is simply a necessary condition for the existence of a law. At present this latter opinion seems to be held by the greater number of the authors, although the former opinion is by no means abandoned. At the present time, both opinions have able defenders, so that it would be very rash to label either of the opinions as untenable, or to deprecate the arguments presented by either group as altogether unconvincing.

Since this controversy of necessity postulates a sharp distinction between the terms essence and condition, it seems properly indicated here to preface the discussion with a few philosophical notes concerning these two concepts. Essence is that by which a thing is what it is. It is that by which a thing is constituted in its proper genus and species, and that which is signified by the definition which states what the thing is.[20] Thus the essence is the most fundamental reality of a thing; it is the source of all the properties and activities of that thing. Philosophers distinguish between the physical essence, which is the thing considered as it is conceived actually to exist in being, and the metaphysical essence, which is the thing considered after the manner in which it is apprehended and defined by our intellects through generic and differentiating concepts.[21]

[19] Cf. Vermeersch, *Theologiae Moralis Principia-Responsa-Consilia* (4 vols., Vol. I, 3.ed., Roma: Pont. Univ. Gregoriana, 1933), I, n. 161.

[20] "Illud per quod res constituitur in proprio genere et specie, et quod significamus per definitionem indicantem, quid est res."—St. Thomas Aquinas, *De Ente et Essentia*, cap. 1; Coffey, *Ontology* (New York: Peter Smith, 1938), p. 75.

[21] Coffey, *Ontology*, p. 75.

A condition in the strict sense of a necessary condition (*conditio sine qua non*)[22] denotes a requisite or a disposition which, although not itself a cause, is necessary that the cause be able to exercise its function of causality. It points to something which must be fulfilled or realized before the effect can be produced or the event can happen. There is a real dependence of the effect on the condition, but the condition itself offers no real and positive influence on the effect.[23]

Very many authors, especially among the older canonists and moralists (although there are a number of modern authors, too, who hold this opinion), held that the act of promulgation is an essential element of law.[24] Their reasons for holding this are:

1. In order that a law be fully constituted, it must impose an actual obligation, since it is of the very nature of law to exist as a binding norm. But a law can not impose any obligation until it has been promulgated. Until it is promulgated, then, a law is not fully constituted in its essence; it is not a true law. It must be concluded, therefore, that promulgation pertains to the essence of law, for what is necessary to constitute something in its essence is certainly essential to it.[25]

---

22 In the present context the term "necessary condition" is always used as a rendition of the Latin "*conditio sine qua non.*"

23 Cf. Gredt, *Elementa Philosophiae Aristotelico-Thomisticae* (7.ed., 2 vols., Friburgi Brisgoviae: Herder, 1937), II, 146; Coffey, *Ontology*, p. 358.

24 The authors who favor this opinion are: Pre-Code: Ballerini, *Opus Theologicum Morale* (Absolvit et edidit Dominicus Palmieri, 7 vols., Prati, 1889-1893), I, 262; Barbosa, *Collectanea Doctorum in Jus Pontificium Universum*, V, 22; Bonacina, *Opera Omnia*, II, Tract. XII, disp. 1, q. 1, punct. 4, n. 6; Bouquillon, *Theologia Moralis Fundamentalis*, p. 270; Leurenius, *Jus Canonicum Universum*, I, 22; Navarrus, *Opera Omnia*, V, 5; Pichler, *Candidatus Jurisprudentiae Sacrae*, Lib. I, Tit. II, n. 16; Santi, *Praelectiones Juris Canonici* (5 vols. in 2, New York, 1886), I, 18; Suarez, *De Legibus*, Lib. I, c. xi, n. 3; Sylvius, *Commentarium in Summam Theologicam S. Thomae Aquinatis* (ed. novissima, 4 vols., Venetiis, 1726), in I.II, q. 90, a. 4, quaer. I; Van Espen, *Scripta Omnia* (4 vols., Lovanii, 1753), IV, 128, *Tractatus de Promulgatione Legum Ecclesiasticarum*, Pars I, cap. 1, §1; Vasquez, *Commentariorum ac Disputationum in Primam Secundae Sancti Thomae Tomus Secundus*, disp. 155, c. 2, n. 16; Vecchiotti, *Institutiones Canonicae*, I, 32. Barbosa lists a score of others who held this opinion, and other lists of proponents of this theory can be found in Sylvius, *loc. cit.*, Michiels, *Normae Generales Juris Canonici*, p. 155, and Van Hove, *Commentarium Lovaniense in Codicem Iuris Canonici*, Vol. I, Tom. II, *De Legibus Ecclesiasticis* (Mechliniae et Romae: Dessain, 1930), p. 114 (hereafter cited as *De Legibus*); Post-Code: Berutti, *Institutiones Iuris Canonici* (6 vols., Vol. I, Taurini-Romae: Marietti, 1936), I, 64; Ferreres, *Institutiones Canonicae* (2.ed., 2 vols., Barcinone, 1920), I, 54; Michiels, *Normae Generales Juris Canonici*, I, 156; Raus, *Institutiones Canonicae* (2.ed., Lugduni, Parisiis: Vitte, 1931), p. 40; Regatillo, *Institutiones Iuris Canonici* (2 vols., Santander: Sal Terrae, Vol. I, 2.ed., 1946, Vol. II, 1942), I, 46; Rodrigo, *De Legibus*, p. 153; Vermeersch-Creusen, *Epitome Iuris Canonici*, I, 52; Wernz-Vidal, *Ius Canonicum*, I, 188.

25 Suarez, *De Legibus*, Lib. I, c. xi, n. 3; Wernz-Vidal, *Ius Canonicum*, I, 189; Michiels, *Normae Generales Juris Canonici*, I, 156.

2. Saint Thomas and Suarez both appropriately include the notion of promulgation in their definition of a law. Whatever is thus included in the definition of a law must exist as an intrinsic and constituent element of it.[26] Saint Thomas explicity stated that the essence of a thing is signified by the definition which states what the thing is.[27]
3. From canon 8, §1, it is to be inferred that the promulgation of a law pertains to the constituting of the law, so much so that it is an essential element of law. By saying that laws are instituted when they are promulgated, the Code implies that the essence of law is not realized until the ordinance is made public by promulgation.
4. A true law is essentially a public norm of action which binds the community. It is not possible for a law to exist solely in the mind of the lawgiver. A law does not consist in a legislator's simple command conceived in his internal will, or even in a command manifested externally to the subjects without any solemnity, but a law is essentially a norm which is obligatory because it has actually been imposed on the community as such by the lawmaker. In order that a rule or a norm be imposed on the community as such, there is an inherent demand of promulgation, since promulgation is the only suitable means by which the law can be levied on the community. Just as in business an external manifestation of consent pertains to the essence of a contract, so the public manifestation of the will of the lawmaker pertains to the essence of law.
5. It is possible to distinguish between active and passive promulgation. The former is the transitory act by which a law is made known to the subjects. This act does not constitute the law and does not pertain to the essence of the law. But passive promulgation, the result of the active promulgation, is in very fact the element which gives public existence to the law (*ipsum esse publicum*). It is this latter promulgation which is an essential element of law, for it is the public norm, made so by being promulgated, that imposes an obli-

[26] Wernz-Vidal, *Ius Canonicum*, I, 188.
[27] *De Ente et Essentia*, cap. 1.

> gation. This public nature of the law is as permanent as the law itself, for once the law has become public, it keeps its public nature.[28]

On the other hand, a number of authors have maintained that promulgation does not belong to the essence of law, and that it is but an extrinsic element of law, a condition which is necessary in order that the essence of law be produced. This opinion is one of long standing, but it seems that in the early days of the controversy it did not have the support that the opposite opinion had, so that most of the authors held that promulgation does pertain to the essence of law. But during the last century the number of authors in support of this second theory has grown considerably. Since the Code there are more authors who hold this opinion than who hold that promulgation pertains to essence of law.[29]

The principal arguments proposed by the authors who favor this opinion are as follows:

1. For the essence of a law it is not necessary that the law actually impose an obligation, but it is merely required that it have an aptitude or a fitness to be of a directive and obligatory character. An ordinance of a lawmaker can have this aptitude before it has been promulgated. Therefore, the

---

[28] Wernz-Vidal, *Ius Canonicum*, I, 189; Michiels, *Normae Generales Juris Canonici*, I, 157, ftn. 2.

[29] The authors in favor of this opinion are: Pre-Code: Billuart, *Summa Summae S. Thomae*, II, 226; D'Annibale, *Summula Theologiae Moralis* (3.ed., 3 vols., Romae, 1892), I, n. 162, nt. 16; De Meester, *Juris Canonici et Juris Canonico-Civilis Compendium* (ed. nova, 3 vols. in 4, Brugis: Desclée De Brouwer, 1921-1928), I, 175; Gonet, *Clypeus Theologiae Thomisticae* (5 vols., Parisiis, 1876), IV, 460; Wernz, *Ius Decretalium* (2.ed., 6 vols., Romae et Prati, 1906-1913), I, n. 100; Post-Code: Chelodi, *Ius Canonicum de Personis*, p. 101; Cicognani, *Canon Law*, p. 544; Cocchi, *Commentarium in Codicem Iuris Canonici* (8 vols. in 5, Taurinorum Augustae: Marietti, 1930-1940), Lib. I, 163; Coronata, *Institutiones Iuris Canonici* (5 vols., Vol. I, 2.ed., Taurini: Marietti, 1939), I, 19; Maroto, *Institutiones Iuris Canonici* (2 vols., Vol. I, 3.ed., Romae, 1921), I, n. 188; Merkelbach, *Summa Theologiae Moralis*, I, 212; Ojetti, *Commentarium in Codicem Iuris Canonici* (4 vols., Romae: Apud Aedes Universitatis Gregorianae, 1927-1931), I, 80; Pruemmer, *Manuale Theologiae Moralis* (5.ed., 3 vols., Friburgi Brisgoviae: Herder, 1928), I, 134; Sipos, *Enchiridion Iuris Canonici*, p. 18. The names of Zallinger, Beste, Blat and Van Hove do not appear in either list, since these authors do not commit themselves to either opinion. Woywod and Augustine do not even mention the controversy. It will be noted that Wernz appears listed among those who maintain that promulgation is only a necessary condition for the binding power of the law, while in the post-Code edition of his work by Vidal the opposite opinion is defended. It is hard to say which side Cappello holds. He makes a unique distinction which could allow a ready commitment to either of the two opinions. He decares that if a law is considered in its complete and formal essence, then promulgation belongs to the essence of law; otherwise, not.—Cappello, *Summa Iuris Canonici* (3 vols., Vol. I, 3.ed., Romae; Aedes Universitatis Gregorianae, 1938), I, n. 70.

whole essence of law can be realized before promulgation, so that promulgation is simply a condition necessary that the law be capable of imposing an actual obligation.[30]

Merkelbach presents an argument similar to this, but phrased in a much more satisfactory manner. He states that, since a law is the command of a superior, it derives its power from his authority, and thus becomes fitted for the imposing of an obligation, so that the obligation results from the promulgation not as from a cause, but as from a necessary condition.[31]

2. A law is a norm or a rule *(regula)* by which one is put under moral constraint either to perform an action or to forego an action. Now, promulgation is not a norm or a rule, nor is it any part of a norm. Hence it cannot be a constituent part of law. It must then be extrinsic to the law.[32]
3. Saint Thomas declared that the act of promulgation is the application of a rule to those who are ruled. This application of the rule does not pertain to the essence of the rule, since it presupposes a rule already constituted which is to be applied. When Saint Thomas taught that the law must be promulgated in order to have the power to bind, he meant the power to bind *in actu secundo,* not *in actu primo.*[33]
4. Promulgation is a transitory act; law is an abiding fact. Therefore, it is not possible that promulgation be an element of the essence of law, since it cannot have a continued co-existence with the law itself.

In further proof of their theory, those who hold that promulgation is not essential to the notion of law offer these answers to the arguments of their opponents:

1. A law to be fully constituted must impose an obligation, and to impose an obligation it must be promulgated. But to

30 Billuart, *Summa Summae S. Thomae,* II, 226; Gonet, *Clypeus Theologiae Thomisticae,* IV, 461.

31 *Summa Theologiae Moralis,* I, 212.

32 Billuart, *loc. cit.;* Maroto, *Institutiones Iuris Canonici,* I, 194; Coronata, *Institutiones Iuris Canonici,* I, 19.

33 Billuart, *Summa Summae S. Thomae,* II, 226; Gonet, *Clypeus Theologiae Thomisticae,* IV, 461; Merkelbach, *Summa Theologiae Moralis,* I, 212.

deduce from this that promulgation is a part of the essence of law is not defensible, since a full explanation is available through the fact that promulgation is simply a necessary condition for the production of a law. It can readily be seen from what has been said about the nature of a necessary condition that a thing can be absolutely necessary for the production of an essence, and still not be part of the essence.

2. In a definition there can rightfully be included not only what pertains to the formal essence of the thing, but also what is a necessary condition that the essence be produced.[34]
3. It is certainly not true that the words of the Code prove that promulgation belongs to the essence of law. They do not even imply this, for even though promulgation be considered merely a necessary condition for the existence of a law, it still remains true that a law can not be instituted until it has been promulgated.
4. It is argued by the opposition that a law is essentially a norm which is actually obligatory because it has been imposed on the community as such by the lawmaker, and that therefore the promulgation of the law is essential to the law. But this is not a valid deduction. The fact that promulgation is necessary for the binding power of the law does not mean that it has to be an essential constituent of the law itself.

On the contrary, those who maintain that promulgation is of the essence of law can offer rebuttals to the arguments advanced by those who declare that promulgation is not a constituent element of law, but merely a necessary condition that the law obtain its binding power.

1. It cannot be admitted that for the essence of law a mere aptitude to establish an obligation is sufficient. A law is essentially a norm or a measure that imposes an obligation. It is not possible, then, for the essence of law to be realized before the law is instituted and begins to bind, i. e., before it has been promulgated.

[34] Cf. Gonet, *Clypeus Theologiae Thomisticae*, IV, 462; Lijdsman, *Introductio in Jus Canonicum* (Hilversum in Hollandia: Sumptibus Societatis Editricis Pontificiae Anonymae, olim Paulus Brand, 1924-1929), p. 412, ft.1.

2. It is true that a law is a norm or a measure, and that promulgation is neither a norm nor a part of a norm. But not any and every norm or measure is a law; only that norm or measure which actually imposes at least an objective obligation can be called a law. The norm or measure becomes a law only when it is applied to the community. So it is by promulgation that the notion of law receives its effective completion.
3. A discussion of what Saint Thomas held in this matter will be given later, but the fact that he taught that promulgation is the application of a rule to those who are ruled can not be offered as proof that promulgation does not belong to the essence of law on grounds that promulgation presupposes the rule as already constituted. There is a distinction to be made between a rule and a law; not every rule is a law, and, although the legislator has constituted some rule of action, it can at best be called the proposal of a law as long as it has not actually become a law through its promulgation.
4. It is possible to distinguish between active and passive promulgation. Active promulgation is the act by which the law becomes public; it is a transitory act. Passive promulgation is the *ipsum esse publicum* of the law, the public nature of the law, which nature is permanent once the active promulgation has taken place. It is this public nature of the ordinance which constitutes it as a law. The active promulgation remains in a moral way.[35]

Before the merits of these two opinions are discussed the teaching of Saint Thomas in this matter should be determined. Authors on both sides quote Saint Thomas in favor of the theory which they hold, e. g., Gonet argued from Saint Thomas that promulgation was a necessary condition, but not an essential element of law.[36]

---

[35] Wernz-Vidal, *Ius Canonicum*, I, 189, 190; Michiels, *Normae Generales Juris Canonici*, I, 156, ftn. 2.

[36] *Clypeus Theologiae Thomisticae*, IV, 461.

Most authors, like Suarez,[37] think that Saint Thomas held that promulgation was of the essence of law. And the words of Saint Thomas himself warrant that conclusion. For the opening words of the article on promulgation[38] are: "Videtur quod promulgatio non est de ratione legis." These words indicate that Saint Thomas was setting out to prove the opposite of this, and therefore that he held that promulgation does belong to the essence of law. Secondly, Saint Thomas himself says that an essence is that by which a thing is constituted in its proper genus and species, and that which is signified by the definition which states what the thing is.[39] Then when speaking of law, he included the notion of promulgation in the definition of law, thus indicating that he maintained that promulgation does pertain to the essence of law.[40] Therefore, although there may not be conclusive proof that Saint Thomas did hold that promulgation belongs to the essence of law, still the indications are that this was the case, and so the writer does not think that those authors are justified who argue from the words of Saint Thomas that promulgation is simply a necessary condition for the existence of law.

The arguments in the foregoing pages as presented by the various authors on both sides can be analysed further. This further analysis will pave the way to arriving at a clearer notion regarding which of the arguments prove the stronger and more compelling. With that object achieved, it will then seem warranted to indicate which of the two opinions stands as the more probably correct one.

Some of the arguments that were presented by the authors to prove that promulgation is an extrinsic element of law and not part of the essence of law cannot be accepted. There are those who argue that to realize the essence of law it is not necessary that a real obligation be imposed, but merely that the norm have an aptitude or fitness for establishing an obligation. That would make the promulgation of the law merely the application of a law already constituted in its essence. But this argument cannot be

[37] *De Legibus*, Lib. I, c. xi, n. 3. Others are Berutti, *Institutiones Iuris Canonici*, I, 64; Van Hove, *De Legibus*, p. 114; Ferreres, *Institutiones Canonicae*, I, 54.

[38] *Summa Theologica*, I.II., q. 90, a. 4, obj. 1.

[39] *De Ente et Essentia*, cap. 1.

[40] *Summa Theologica*, I.II., q. 90, a. 4, in corp.

accepted, since the essence of law demands that an actual obligation be imposed. This is not accomplished before the law is instituted. Hence the promulgation of the law is necessary in order that the essence of law be realized. If it is not necessary as a constitutent element of law, it is at least a necessary condition for the production of the law.

It does not seem admissible, as was shown above, to cite Saint Thomas as favoring the non-essence theory regarding promulgation. It was very probably such poor arguments as the two just mentioned that to a great extent caused this opinion to be less popular among the earlier authors. But the modern exponents of the non-essence theory defend it with arguments that are more acceptable.

In favor of their opinion it can be said that it offers a much more simple explanation of the relationship of promulgation to the essence of law, and the statement that promulgation is but a necessary condition is quite in keeping with the doctrine of the Code.[41] Especially as it is put by Maroto (1875-1937), this argument seems convincing. He says that when promulgation is said to be a necessary condition, what is meant is that promulgation is so necessary that without it a law cannot be produced.[42] This saves the absolute necessity of promulgation, and at the same time offers an effective safeguard against falling into the error that the essence of law is realized before promulgation. According to this argument, therefore, even though promulgation is not an intrinsic element of the essence of law, still the essence of law cannot be produced until the law has been promulgated. The strongest argument in favor of the opinion of Maroto seems to be that which was presented as the second argument above, namely, that promulgation is neither a rule nor a part of a rule; so it can not be a part of the essence of law. And yet the opponents of this theory have a good answer to that argument, too.

By no means, however, can one regard as apodictic all the arguments presented by those who hold that promulgation is an essential element of law. Especially the older authors offered proofs that were not always convincing. Many of their arguments

[41] Canon 8, §1.
[42] Maroto, *Institutiones Iuris Canonici*, I, 193.

did not exclude the possibility that promulgation could also be but a necessary condition, so that they proved, not that promulgation is an essential element of law, but rather that it is absolutely necessary for the existence of the law. But in consideration of the nature of law and in the light of the explanation of modern authors[43] regarding the manner in which promulgation pertains to the essence of law, it is the essence theory concerning the concept of promulgation that appeals to the writer as the preferable doctrine.

A distinction certainly can be made between active and passive promulgation. Passive promulgation pertains to the essence of law, since it is essential that the law be a public obligatory norm of action, i. e., a promulgated norm of action. This explains more perfectly and explicitly what the older authors evidently meant, although they did not state it with the fullest measure of clarity. Another strong point for this opinion is the argument from authority, for the weight of great authority supports this theory, especially since Saint Thomas most probably and Suarez certainly held it.

The one thing that is evident in this controversy is that, although both groups offer what appears to be an adequate explanation of the relation of promulgation to the notion of law, neither one can prove conclusively that their opinion is to be held to the exclusion of the other. There is no proof offered that establishes one position as certainly to be held to the absolute exclusion of the other.

Article 3

The Extension of the Necessity of the Element of the Promulgation of a Law

The purpose of this article is to answer the question, what must be promulgated? In general it can be said that promulgation is required for all laws, i. e., for all norms which impose a new obligation on the community. Promulgation, therefore, is necessary not only for affirmative and negative laws, for per-

[43] Cf. especially Michiels, *Normae Generales Juris Canonici,* I, 156 sqq.; and Wernz-Vidal, *Ius Canonicum,* I, 188 sqq.

missive and penal legislation, which types of law involve primarily the factors of guilt and penalty, but also for invalidating and incapacitating laws. In other words, all human laws must be promulgated.

1.

Natural Law

It has been shown that every law needs promulgation, but the question regarding the promulgation of natural law presents a difficulty. It is not immediately evident how the natural law has been promulgated by God, since there seems to be no act of God by which the natural law has been presented to the subjects as a body in order to inform them that the supreme Legislator intends to bind them by this ordinance. In the first place, it is to be noted that the predication of the term law when applied to human and natural law is an analogous predication, and consequently the promulgation of the natural law will not have to be exactly the same as that of human law.

It is the common opinion that knowledge or notice of the natural law is had merely by the acquisition of a rational nature through generation, for with human nature comes the light of reason, although initially impeded, along with which the natural law is also received from the Author of nature. So the natural law is made known to us through reason.[44]

Suarez taught that the natural law is promulgated by the fact that it flows from nature itself. According to him it arises from the specific essence of man's nature. Though the publication of the natural law seems to be made to individuals, it is not a proposition that is directed to each particular person as an individual, but it is the voice of God speaking as a public Person, as the Author of all nature.[45]

It may be concluded that a sufficient promulgation of the natural law was had at the creation of Adam, for by the creation of Adam God created human nature in the head of the human race, and human nature descends from Adam to his individual

[44] Cf. Rodrigo, *De Legibus*, p. 156.
[45] Suarez, *De Legibus*, Lib. I, c. xi, n. 4.

descendants through human generation. Since each man receives the natural law with his human nature, it can be said that with the creation of Adam the natural law was promulgated by being presented to Adam who represented the entire human race. So the reception of the natural law by an individual is merely the extension of the promulgation that already was made to mankind through Adam its progenitor.[46]

2.

Invalidating and Incapacitating Laws

Promulgation is required for all laws, i. e., for all norms imposing an obligation on the public. This necessity extends to invalidating and incapacitating laws. It may seem that such laws do not need promulgation, since their effect is not dependent on the knowledge of the subjects, for such laws bind even those who are ignorant of them.[47] But these laws are true laws, and as such they must be presented to the public; they must be promulgated. The community has a right to know how it can perform its actions so that they will be valid, and so it is necessary that laws affecting the validity of acts be presented to the community in such a way that it is possible for all the members to know of the law. It would be too grave a burden on the community if these laws did not need promulgation.

It may also seem that retroactive invalidating or incapacitating laws bind before promulgation, else they would not be retroactive. But such laws do not exert any force before the time that they are promulgated. It is only when they have been promulgated that they have the force of law, and then they begin to have a retroactive effect, so that they affect acts placed before the promulgation of the law.

3.

Interpretations of Law

In canon 17, §2, the Code deals with the promulgation of authentic interpretations of law, and it states that an authentic

[46] Rodrigo, *De Legibus*, p. 157.
[47] Canon 16, §1.

interpretation of law given in the manner of a law has the same force as the law itself, and that the interpretation which merely declares the meaning of the words of the law which were in themselves certain does not need to be promulgated and moreover is retroactive in its effect. But, if the interpretation restricts or extends the law, or explains a doubtful law, then the interpretation is not retroactive in its effect, but necessarily looks to an act of promulgation for acquiring its desired juridical force and effect.[48]

An authentic interpretation is one which is made by the author of the law, by his successor, or by a delegate of either of these.[49] The various kinds of authentic interpretations as listed in canon 17, §2, are designated by the authors as follows:

a. A declarative or comprehensive interpretation is one which explains the words of a law which is in itself certain and clear;

b. An explanatory or clarifying interpretation is one which elucidates really doubtful terms of the law;

c. An extensive interpretation is one which amplifies the law to include cases which would not ordinarily be included by the terms of the law;

d. A restrictive interpretation is one which limits the applicatory norm of a law by removing from its scope cases which are really included according to the words of the law.[50]

To decide whether or not these various types of interpretation need promulgation, one must simply decide whether or not they constitute new legislation. Since in the case of a merely declarative interpretation no new obligation is imposed by the interpretation, it is not necessary that it be promulgated.[51] The explanatory or clarifying interpretation, which solves a real

---

[48] "Interpretatio authentica, per modum legis exhibita, eandem vim habet ac lex ipsa; et si verba legis in se certa declaret tantum, promulgatione non eget et valet retrorsum; si legem coarctet vel extendat aut dubiam explicet, non retrotrahitur et debet promulgari."

[49] Canon 17, §1: "Leges authentice interpretatur legislator eiusve successor et is cui potestas interpretandi fuerit ab eisdem commissa."

[50] Cf. Cicognani, *Canon Law*, p. 601; Wernz-Vidal, *Ius Canonicum*, I, 228; Coronata, *Institutiones Iuris Canonici*, I, 36; Beste, *Introductio in Codicem* (2.ed., Collegeville: St. John's Abbey Press, 1944), p. 76.

[51] Canon 17, §2.

doubt of law, is really new law, and as such it must be promulgated.[52] Until the authentic interpretation is given there is no obligation in this case, for a doubtful law does not bind. The Code in this instance has settled a controversy that existed among pre-Code authors. A majority of the canonists before the Code contended that such a solution of a doubt was a merely declarative interpretation, for they thought that it really only disclosed or made manifest what was already contained in the law.[53]

This controversy was not directly concerned with the notion of the promulgation of law. The object of this controversy was to decide whether the interpretation of a really doubtful law constituted a new law, or merely furnished a more clear statement of what was already contained in the extant law. The conclusion or decision regarding the necessity of the promulgation of such an interpretation depended on the answer to that problem, since all admitted that, if the interpretation implied the constituting of a new law, promulgation was necessary. From paragraph two of canon 17 it is clear that both the extensive and the restrictive authentic interpretations of law are to be classed as interpretations which impose a new obligation, and therefore they do need promulgation.[54]

Related to the question of the promulgation of the interpretations of law is the historical controversy concerning the legal value of the decrees of the Roman Congregations. Before the issuance of the Constitution "*Sapienti Consilio*" of Pope Pius X, on June 29, 1908, it was the interpretations rendered by the Sacred Congregation of the Council that were the principal subject of controversy. This Congregation had been established by papal authority to interpret the decrees of the Council of Trent. Whether the decrees of this Congregation had the force of universal law when they had not been promulgated by apostolic authority was greatly disputed by the canonists of the

---

[52] Canon 17, §2.

[53] Cf. Cicognani, *Canon Law*, p. 605.

[54] Schmidt, *The Principles of Authentic Interpretation in Canon 17 of the Code of Canon Law*, The Catholic University of America Canon Law Studies, n. 141 (Washington, D. C.: The Catholic University of America Press, 1941), p. 219.

pre-Code era. Some of the declarations of this Sacred Congregation were confirmed and promulgated by papal decree. Concerning these there was no argument; they were certainly universally binding. Some of the decrees were not promulgated. If they contained interpretations of law which were extensive or restrictive in character, so that they affected a change in the original law by adding to it or taking away from it, then the decrees were just as certainly not universally binding, since they equivalently implied the existence of a new law, which like any other new legislation demanded an act of promulgation, if they were to have binding force. On this, too, there was common agreement.[55]

The controversy, therefore, concerned simply those decrees or declarations which merely explained the sense of the law without making changes, and were not promulgated. Some authors denied that such declarations of the Sacred Congregations had the force of universal law when they had not been promulgated, and hence considered them binding only in the case for which they were given.[56]

But according to Schmalzgrueber (1663-1735)[57] and many others[58] the comprehensive (merely declarative) decrees of the Sacred Congregation of the Council did not need promulgation in order to have the force of universal legislation, for the simple reason that they were not new laws. A law needed solemn promulgation only when it was first made, and after that it was binding. These decrees did not in any way change the extant law, but merely explained the real sense of the law, and so did not constitute new law and hence needed no solemn promulgation to be binding generally. Once it was established that decrees of the Congregations entailed the enactment of new laws, or at least equivalently amounted to new laws inasmuch as they

---

[55] Bouix, *Tractatus de Curia Romana* (Parisiis, 1859), p. 301 (hereafter cited as *De Curia Romana*).

[56] Bouix (*De Curia Romana*, p. 304) stated that Sanchez (1550-1610), Diana (1585-1663) and Laymann (1574-1635) favored this opinion. Bonacina (†1631) definitely did uphold it: *Opera Omnia*, II, Tract. XII, disp. 1, quaes. 1, punct. 8, n. 4.

[57] *Jus Ecclesiasticum Universum*, Dissertatio Proemialis, §IX, n. 376.

[58] E.g., Reiffenstuel (*Jus Canonicum Universum* [5 vols. in 7, Parisiis, 1864-1870], Proemium, n. 133) and the authors to whom he adverts.

extended or restricted the former law, then the decrees in order to become binding had to be promulgated.

4.
Precepts

A precept is a particular command given by a competent superior for either the common good of a group or the private good of an individual. It has this in common with a law that it is a norm which imposes an obligation, but it differs from a law in that it is a particular command given to an individual as such, or, if given to a community, it is in reference simply to a particular case.[59]

A precept is not a law, but it is analogous to the law, since it has a number of things in common with a law. Since it does impose an obligation, a precept must be made known to the subject or subjects for whom it is intended, and this announcement must be made on the authority of the one who enjoins the precept. It is not promulgation that is required here, since the announcement is not directed toward the community as a body, but rather something analogous to promulgation is demanded, and this is called the announcement *(intimatio)* of the precept. The precept does not bind until the notice of the precept has been received by the subjects. Consequently this announcement of the precept is necessary in order that the precept have a binding force in the external forum as well as in the internal forum.[60] Precepts are said to be given, and this giving is to the precept as promulgation is to a law.

The Code in canon 24 establishes the procedure to be followed by the preceptor when he announces a precept to an individual if he desires to have the right to urge the fulfillment of the precept in court. In order that the preceptor be able to urge in court the fulfillment of the precept he must impose the precept either by means of a legitimate document or before two witnesses. Furthermore, if the preceptor gives his precept in either of the ways mentioned in canon 24, the binding force of

---

59 Rodrigo, *De Legibus*, p. 19; Cicognani, *Canon Law*, p. 636.
60 Cf. Rodrigo, *De Legibus*, p. 458.

the precept continues even after the preceptor has gone out of power.[61]

5.

Customary Law

By a customary law is meant that kind of law which has been introduced by the long-standing habits and usage of the community with the approval of a competent superior. In this discussion there are contemplated, not customs which have been formed and approved though they run counter to the written statues of law, but rather those which exist outside or beyond the pale of the law *(praeter legem)*, namely those which have introduced new legal obligations. These are the customs treated in canon 28.

As is evident, a customary law differs somewhat from a written or an oral law of a superior. A written law originates in the lawmaker, a customary law from a factual usage existing in the community. The Code plainly indicates that no such factual usage can obtain the force of customary law in the church except from the consent of a competent ecclesiastical superior.[62] Guilfoyle explains that this consent can be given in a special way by means of approval expressed by words or signs, or by means of approval indicated by the silence of the legislator. Or the competent superior can give what is known as legal consent by establishing beforehand, as the Holy See has done in canons 27 and 28, conditions which must be fulfilled if some practice or usage on the part of the community is to obtain the force of law. The superior then states in effect that he approves any and every custom that measures up to these conditions.[63]

A customary law differs from a written law also regarding the matter of promulgation. The legal or formal element of a customary law is intimated and promulgated by means of the written law which acknowledges the character and regulates

61 "Praecepta, singulis data, eos quibus dantur, ubique urgent, sed iudicialiter urgeri nequeunt et cessant resoluto iure praecipientis, nisi per legitimum documentum aut coram duobus testibus imposita fuerint."

62 Canon 25: "Consuetudo in Ecclesia vim legis a consensu competentis Superioris ecclesiastici unice obtinet."

63 Guilfoyle, *Custom*, The Catholic University of America Canon Law Studies, n. 105 (Washington, D. C.: The Catholic University of America, 1937), p. 83.

the status of customary law.[64] By the very fact that the community's practice and usage measures up to the conditions set by the legislator, the latter presents the established custom to the community as a law, though he does not then and there resort explicitly to any formal act wherewith to intimate the customary law to the community. Zallinger (1735-1813) called this a tacit promulgation,[65] and Bouquillon declared the act of announcement or intimation to be implicit in the very formation of the customary law.[66]

As far as the passive promulgation is concerned, there arises no problem regarding the public existence of a customary law which has arisen from an approved usage. The material element of such a law is the factual usage current among the subjects, so there can be no question of the public nature and character of such a law. Guilfoyle, however, states that there is no element of promulgation relative to customary law.[67] By that he evidently means that no explicit act of promulgation such as that which is prescribed in canon 9 is needed. For customary law as well as for a written or an oral law there must be an act of promulgation, but this act differs from the promulgation of a written or an oral law in the way mentioned above.

6.
Privileges

Privilege can be taken in the wide sense to include the clerical privileges. These, since they are laws, must be promulgated. But the necessity of promulgation arises from the fact that they are laws, and not from the fact that they are privileges. Such privileges need to be promulgated only because of their inseparable connection and intimate identification with the concept of law.

But privilege is usually taken in the strict sense of the concession of some special right made by a legitimate superior.[68] In the case of a privilege in the strict sense promulgation is not

64 Rodrigo, *De Legibus*, p. 463.

65 *Institutiones Juris Ecclesiastici*, I, 118.

66 *Theologia Moralis Fundamentalis*, p. 270.

67 *Custom*, p. 85.

68 "Privilegium est concessio alicuius iuris specialis a legitimo superiore facta."—Roelker, *Principles of Privilege according to the Code of Canon Law*, The Catholic University of America Canon Law Studies, n. 35 (Washington, D. C.: The Catholic University of America, 1926), p. 16.

necessary, since such a concession is not a law, not even as some have defined it, a private law.[69] The privilege should be brought to the notice of the grantee, but the validity of the privilege does not postulate this notice or any solemn announcement of the grant by the superior.

7.

Chancery Regulations

The Rules of the Chancery (*Regulae Cancellariae*) were papal regulations relating to the conduct of business in the Roman Curia. During the pontificate of the Pope who had approved and promulgated them they had the force of law. They were concerned with the delegation of judges and with the granting of benefices, privileges, indults, dispensations, etc. Since the Chancery dates back many years before Pope John XXII (1316-1334), there were certainly norms which governed the Papal Chancery before his time, but he was the first to reduce them to form and to put them in writing. They were reformed by Gregory XI (1370-1378), corrected by Urban VI (1378-1389), and put into their present form, except for slight changes made by later popes, by Nicholas V in 1450.[70]

Some authors held that these Chancery Rules were not true laws, but the common opinion now is that certainly many of them were laws. They did not differ from the constitutions of the popes, since they were papal decrees concerning certain matters of general discipline. They had the force of universal law and were a source of Canon Law.

The reason for the separate consideration of these Chancery Rules is that there is a problem concerning the promulgation of these regulations. Although these regulations were laws, they were binding *in actu secundo* only during the reign of the pope who had promulgated them, and they were considered as not imposing any subjective obligation from the time of the death of that pontiff until they were approved by his successor. The

---

[69] E.g., Suarez, *De Legibus*, Lib. VIII, c. i, n. 3.

[70] Van Hove, *Commentarium Lovaniense in Codicem Iuris Canonici*, Vol. I, Tom. I, *Prolegomena* (2.ed., Mechliniae et Romae: H. Dessain, 1945), p. 378, n. 383 (hereafter cited as *Prolegomena*); Cicognani, *Canon Law*, p. 323.

approbation by the newly elected pope came before his consecration, on the day after his election. The Chancery Regulations which had been in force during the reign of the previous pope were declared to be binding from the moment of approbation, even before they were solemnly promulgated in the Apostolic Chancery, where they were read in the presence of the Cardinal Vice-Chancellor, the prelates, and other officials of the Chancery. New regulations had to be promulgated before they were binding.

It was Pope Urban VIII (1623-1644) who first proclaimed them binding from the moment of papal approbation even prior to their solemn promulgation. In his Bull "*Sanctissimus in Christo,*" issued on August 7, 1623, there is found the following introduction:

> "Sanctissimus in Christo Pater et D.N.D. Urbanus divina providentia Papa VIII, suorum praedecessorum vestigiis inhaerendo, normam et ordinem gerendis dare volens, in crastinum suae assumptionis ad summi apostolatus apicem, videlicet die vii mensis augusti, anno ab Incarnatione Domini MDCXXIII, reservationes, constitutiones et regulas infrascriptas fecit, quas etiam ex tunc *licet nondum publicatas*[71] et suo tempore duraturas observari voluit, ac quas nos Ludovicus tituli S. Laurentii in Damaso presbyter Cardinalis Ludovisius S.R.E. vice-cancellarius die xxi mensis octobris dicti anni in cancellaria apostolica publicari fecimus."[72]

After Pope Pius VI (1775-1799) the Chancery Rules were no longer promulgated.

In view of what has been said concerning the necessity of an act of promulgation for the existence of a law, it may seem that the issuance of the Chancery Regulations implied either an exception to the rule, or else a contradiction of the doctrine of the absolute necessity of promulgation. But that this was not so can be seen from the statement of Reiffenstuel (1642-1703), namely, that a new law needed promulgation, but that a solemn promulgation was necessary only when the law was first enacted, and

---

[71] Italics supplied by the writer.

[72] *Bullarum Diplomatum et Privilegiorum Sanctorum Romanorum Pontificum Taurinensis Editio* (24 vols. et Appendix, Augustae Taurinorum—Neapoli, 1857-1872), XIII, 57 (hereafter cited as *Bullarium*).

not when it was again declared.[73] In the case of the Chancery Rules the laws were not revoked on the death of the Pontiff, but they were considered as not imposing a subjective obligation until they were approved by the new pope. The condition of these laws could be compared to that of a law which has been promulgated, but which does not as yet impose a subjective obligation in view of the period of grace (*vacatio legis*) granted by the legislator.

These regulations needed the approbation of each newly elected pope. But promulgation was not necessary, since he merely declared that these same laws were once more binding *in actu secundo*. Further proof of this is the fact that after the time of Pius VI they were no longer solemnly published. It was taken for granted that the new pope would approve the old set of rules, although he might perhaps make slight changes.

With reference to such effected changes or to any new laws which were added during the course of time, no binding obligation resulted before their promulgation. Once they had been promulgated, however, it was possible that they might have retroactive effect. Of course, the retroactive Chancery Rules could not bind in conscience, that is, as far as guilt or penalty was concerned, until they had been publicly promulgated. Only those persons were considered guilty of crime and subject to penalties who, after the promulgation of these new retroactive rules, performed actions contrary to the Chancery Regulations. Acts performed within a period of time prior to the promulgation of the Chancery Rules were affected only in the matter of their validity or invalidity according as they had been performed in accord with or in contravention of the newly promulgated Chancery Regulations. Hence ecclesiastical courts simply decided that acts done prior to the promulgation of the new rules were invalid, even though they had been performed before the Chancery Regulations were promulgated, but the person who performed such acts was not considered guilty of a crime nor was he liable to punishment.

In treating of the Chancery Rules, Castropalao (1581-1633) stated that they were certainly laws, and that accordingly they

[73] *Jus Canonicum Universum*, Lib. III, Tit. V, §xvi, n. 480.

needed to be promulgated if they were to bind as laws. But he explained that these regulations as real laws, indeed obliged everyone, not because they had the force of written laws, but rather because they existed as customary laws. Public usage to which had acceded the consent of the Pontiffs was the equivalent of their promulgation. So, according to Castropalao, the Chancery Rules did not bind as laws until the time when approved usage had evolved to the estate of customary law.[74] From what has been said above it is clear that this was not the case, for the Chancery Rules bound as soon as they were approved by the newly elected Pope. New regulations were binding, too, and not only after the lapse of time necessary before they had evolved to the estate of customary law, but as soon as they had been promulgated by being posted in the Apostolic Chancery.

8.

Revocation of Law

It is disputed among authors whether a law can be revoked by a merely internal act on the part of a competent superior. Some authors insist that a revocation of law must be solemnly announced to the subjects. So on the one hand there are authors who claim that a promulgation of the revocation of a law is as necessary as a promulgation of the law itself. They argue that, since a law is a norm of human action, so also the revocation of a law is a norm, for it permits the opposite of that which was commanded or forbidden by the revoked law. If a law must be promulgated, then a revocation of the law must be promulgated also.

Although Rodrigo[75] lists Vasquez (1549-1604), Sylvius (1581-1649) and Castropalao (1581-1633) as holding this opinion, in all fairness to them it seems that Vasquez and Sylvius did not explicitly teach the doctrine which Rodrigo attributes to them.[76]

---

[74] *Opera Omnia* (7 vols., Lugduni, 1700), Tract. III, disp. 1, punct. 10, n. 6.

[75] *De Legibus*, p. 404, ftn. 8.

[76] Cf. Vasquez, *Commentariorum ac Disputationum in Primam Secundae Sancti Thomae Tomus Secundus*, disp. 156, c. 4, n. 25; Sylvius, *Commentarium in Summam Theologicam S. Thomae Aquinatis*, I.II., q. 96, a. 4, quaer. 13.

Both of these authors, when they demanded the element of promulgation for the revocation of a law, spoke of new laws which were revocatory in character. They did not treat of any other method concerning the revocation of law. With reference to the case wherein a revocation of law is effected in some way other than by the promulgation of a new law, they did not explicitly deny the need of an act of promulgation. Perhaps this accounts for the fact that they are listed by Rodrigo as holding the opinion that in all cases of the revocation of a law an act of promulgation is called for. But neither of them explicitly stated that promulgation is necessary for a direct revocation of a law, that is, for an act of revocation which does not involve and is unaccompanied with the promulgation of a new law revocatory in character. Castropalao certainly should not be included among those who held the opinion that every revocation of law needs a solemn promulgation. His opinion coincided with the doctrine which Suarez held in this matter.[77]

On the other hand, other authors held that a revocation of law need not be promulgated.[78] They argued that more was needed to impose an obligation than to take it away. For the imposing of an obligation many elements had to concur if a law was to become a reality, so that the absence of any one of these elements was sufficient to prevent the law from being instituted, or to undo its existence after it had been instituted. Since the act of revocation of a law did not levy an obligation but simply cancelled out whatever obligation existed, it did not stand in need of all the elements which were necessary for attaching a binding force to the law in the first place. If, then, there was a cessation in the will of the superior to bind his subjects, the law automatically also ceased, even apart from any accompanying solemn pronouncement to that effect.

Suarez himself, not committing himself to either side, made a distinction between the direct revocation of a law and the revocation made by means of the substitution of a new law

[77] *Opera Omnia*, I, Tr. III, disp. 5, punct. 2, nn. 4 & 5.

[78] Some who held this opinion are listed by Suarez, *De Legibus*, Lib. VI, c. xxvii, n. 15.

revoking the old law.[79] He declared that if the revocation followed from a law that was contrary to the existing law, then an act of promulgation was necessary, since there was constituted a new law, which could not be instituted until it had been promulgated. But a direct revocation of law did not inherently require an act of promulgation. It seems clear that, even though Suarez invoked a distinction, he should be numbered among those who held that promulgation was not necessary for the simple revocation of a law. All of the authors who held this opinion, even though they did not mention the necessity of promulgation when the revocation was made by means of a new law contrary to the first one, would naturally have agreed that such a new law needed promulgation.

The opinion of Suarez, which is adopted also by Rodrigo,[80] certainly seems to be the correct one. This conclusion follows from the argument given by those who contend that an act of promulgation is not necessary for the revocation of a law. If the lawmaker has withdrawn his will to levy an obligation, there is no longer any law.

Of course, even though a formal promulgation of the revocation of a law is not necessary for the revocation to take effect, still the act of revocation on the part of the legislator should be made known to his subjects. The community has a right to know when an obligation has ceased, and the cessation of a law is not presumed unless its revocation is externally manifest. Such an announcement to the community can be made in any way; it is not necessary that it be a public announcement to the community as such on the authority of the superior. But Suarez suggested that the announcement of the revocation of a law should be a public act. Prudence in the legislator will naturally incline him to invite public notice in his act of revoking a law. Otherwise scandal could readily result when, to the exclusion of others, certain persons in their private knowledge concerning the revocation of the law are observed as no longer respecting what is still regarded by the general public as an extant law.[81]

---

79 *De Legibus*, Lib. VI, c. xxvii, n. 16; see also Castropalao, *loc. cit.* and Gonet, *Clypeus Theologiae Thomisticae*, IV, 539.

80 *De Legibus*, p. 404.

81 *De Legibus*, Lib. VI, c. xxvii, n. 18.

9.

Dogmatic Definitions

Definitions regarding doctrines of faith or of morals do not of themselves need promulgation. Yet, if they are presented in the form of true laws which oblige the faithful in their external profession of faith, then an act of promulgation is called for in view of the character of law that then attaches to such definitions.

10.

Necessity of the Diocesan Divulgation of a Promulgated Universal Law

It is disputed whether the Code imposes on ordinaries an obligation of divulging in their dioceses the general laws of the Church. Historically this problem derived from the doctrine which upheld the sufficiency of the promulgation of universal ecclesiastical legislation in Rome alone. St. Alphonsus Liguori agreed with Sylvius[82] that bishops were bound to publish universal ecclesiastical laws in their dioceses whenever a papal mandate was issued to that effect, or whenever the bishops could reasonably judge that a publication in their dioceses was necessary. Of course, those who knew of the law were bound by it even before this diocesan divulgation had taken place. In other cases, that is, when the aforementioned conditions were not realized, it was at least probable that the bishops were not under any obligation to make a law known unless from the publication of the law in their dioceses it was to be expected that great fruit would accrue to the Church.[83]

With the issuance of the present Code, Ojetti contended,[84] there was imposed on ordinaries the obligation of divulging general ecclesiastical laws in their dioceses. He argued: 1) from canon 336, §1, that if the ordinary is bound to urge the observance of the laws of the Holy See, he is also bound to publish them in his diocese, and 2) from canon 509, §1, which imposes

---

[82] Sylvius, *Commentarium in Summam Theologicam S. Thomae Aquinatis*, Q. 96, a. 4, quaer. xi, concl. 3.

[83] Alphonsus Maria de Ligorio, *Theologia Moralis*, Lib. I, n. 96.

[84] *Commentarium in Codicem Iuris Canonici*, I, 81.

an obligation on religious superiors of publishing among their subjects the decrees of the Holy See which pertain to religious. Ojetti maintained that if this is prescribed by the Code for religious superiors, then it is evidently the mind of the Code that the same publication of the laws of the Holy See is to be made by local ordinaries among their diocesan subjects.

The arguments alleged by Ojetti certainly do not prove that ordinaries are obliged under the Code to publish in their territories the general laws of the Holy See. Rather, it is better to hold with Van Hove[85] that, since it is the duty of ordinaries according to canon 336, §1, to urge the observance of the general ecclesiastical laws, it will often be expedient, or the proper fulfillment of their office will at times demand, that ordinaries bring notice of the universal ecclesiastical laws to their subjects by means of a wider divulgation. No obligation to make such a divulgation arises from the Code, but an obligation could, of course, be imposed though an express command of the Holy See.

[85] *De Legibus*, p. 138.

PART TWO

The Methods Used for the Promulgation of Laws

For the instituting of a law there suffices that promulgation of the law which is effected by means of an external manifestation of the enacted law to the community in such a way that the entire community can become informed of the law. The nature either of law or of promulgation does not demand that promulgation be effected by means of any standard method. Rather, any method which will put the law before the community in such a way that it becomes humanly possible for the community to obtain knowledge of the law will suffice for its promulgation. The choice of the method is left to the legislator.

During the course of the centuries the methods used by the Church for the promulgation of ecclesiastical law have varied. It is the purpose of the second part of this treatise to discuss the various methods of promulgation used during the centuries since the beginning of the Christian era.

CHAPTER I

The Promulgation of Law Before 538

In the beginning of the Christian era the science of Canon Law was not developed for several reasons. Primarily it was because the Church at first was ruled by the authority of the apostles rather than by means of a juridical structure in the Church. Then, too, the enthusiasm of the early Christians made technical determination seem unnecessary. To them the cultivation of the spiritual life proved all important, so that they were little concerned with the technical formulation of laws. It was not that the law did not exist, but rather that no one stressed its juridical formation.

It stands as a readily recognized fact that throughout the earlier history of the Church the technical notion of promulgation, as developed by the great canonists since the time of Gratian, in the middle of the XII century, was unknown. It is equally evident from the early legal sources that there was a lack of any clear distinction between the mere issuance of a law and its promulgation, or also between the publication of a promulgated law and the initial promulgation. The Roman Law served as a basis of the Canon Law of that period to a great extent, and in the Roman Law there existed many concepts for which there were no technical terms.

Even Justinian (527-565), who issued the first law on promulgation, did not have a clear idea of promulgation as distinct from the solemn issuing of a law, or from its publication after the act of promulgation. This distinction, it seems, did not occur to the legal minds of the time. In his preface to Novella 65, which Novella immediately preceded the Novella which contained his law on promulgation, Justinian used the verb *promulgare* to convey the idea of the issuance of the law. But even so, it was recognized that to be binding a law had to be presented to the public as a precept of the ruling power, and care was accordingly taken that this be done.

Just as it is true that the natural law demands that an enacted law be made known to the community at large, so also it is a fact that the lawmaker is free to choose for the achievement of this task whatever particular method suits his purpose. So ecclesiastical laws from the very beginning of the Church were promulgated, but there was for nineteen centuries no positive general ecclesiastical enactment to prescribe a standard method of promulgation. It remained for the Constitution *Promulgandi* of Pope Pius X (1903-1914) to establish a prescribed uniform method for the promulgating of ecclesiastical laws. Naturally the means used for promulgating ecclesiastical laws differed over the course of so many centuries.

Article 1

Roman Civil Law

Both Theodosius II (408-450) and Justinian I (527-565) frequently used the words *promulgare* and *promulgatio,* but not with the exact meaning which attaches to these words today. They usually employed them to point to the issuance of law, and less frequently to refer to its divulgation after the real promulgation. In the time of Justinian it was the duty of the pretorian prefect to see to it that copies of the imperial constitutions were sent to the proper public officers for promulgation.[1]

When imperial constitutions pertaining to religion were issued, they were sent to the Patriarch of Constantinople with instructions that he should send them to his metropolitans, they in turn to their subject bishops, and these finally to the monasteries.[2] There are only a few cases in which constitutions were sent to other patriarchs and metropolitans besides the Patriarch of Constantinople,[3] including at times the Bishop of Rome.[4]

[1] N. 4, addressed: "Idem Augustus Iohanni gloriosissimo praefecto sacro praetorio." The epilogue reads: "Iam quae in subditorum utilitatem a nobis sancita sunt, eminentia tua cognoscens solitis edictis et hic et per omnes partes imperii manifesta facienda curet. . . ."

[2] N. 5, epil., addressed to Epiphanius, the Patriarch of Constantinople: "Haec igitur omnia sanctissimi patriarchae deo carissimis metropolitanis sibi subditis manifesta reddant, ii vero deo carissimos episcopos ipsis subditos certiores faciant, atque illi cum monasteriis, quae in ipsorum potestate sunt, communicent."

[3] N. 6, epil., is an example.

[4] N. 7, epil.

Justinian ordered that religious laws be published outside the church, but that a copy of them be kept inside with the sacred vessels. It was the Emperor's expressed preference that the law be inscribed on stone tablets at the entrance of the church.[5]

Article 2

Papal Legislation

The Church was born into a Roman world governed by Roman Law. Quite naturally the first rulers of the Christian communities looked to the Roman Law as their guide in legal matters. Furthermore the period of the Church's history from the Edict of Constantine (313) to the sixth century was marked by a close collaboration between Church and State. Each one exerted a great deal of influence on the law of the other. The chief reason for the influence of Roman Law on the Church was that the Church as an institution had to have a system of law. The Roman Law, as the only well developed system at hand, suited the Church's purpose.

Inasmuch as at that time there was no general law of the Church concerning the promulgating of papal and synodal legislation, and because there was no precise notion of the concept of promulgation, no uniform way was used for the promulgating of Church law. The Church looked to Roman Law for its norm in this matter, yet it certainly did not canonize the civil law. It is known that the popes and other bishops were solicitous about the publishing of the laws passed by them or by the local and general synods of that time. They realized that the clergy and laity could not be expected to obey laws which they did not know. Accordingly they took great pains to see to it that notice of the laws did reach the people. However, they certainly did not follow any one method of publication. A study of the documents of the early Church reveals that at least two methods of promulgation were in quite common use.

There was the practice of promulgating laws by means of letters to individual bishops or to several of them along with instructions that they see to the publication of the laws in their

---

[5] N. 8, edictum.

respective territories. These letters were usually sent by clerical messengers, priests or deacons, trusted by the popes. Usually these laws were considered promulgated by the fact that they were sent out in this way to bishops in the various parts of the world. The manner of promulgation within the dioceses varied, but it is clear from the words of Tertullian (ca. 160-ca. 230) that laws were read in the churches at a very early date.[6] Other laws, especially those pertaining to the clergy alone, were divulged in synods, but from the tenor of the letters it is clear that the laws were considered promulgated when they were sent to the bishops, and it then became incumbent on them to see that notice of the new legislation was duly received by those for whom the laws had been enacted. Side by side with the former method there existed another method, that namely of promulgating laws before the assembly of priests and bishops gathered together in synod. That still other ways were used is also evident, but the two methods here mentioned constituted the ordinary methods of promulgation.

Tertullian, writing in the year 221 about a decree which by modern critics is usually attributed to Pope Calixtus I (217-222),[7] namely, that absolution could be given by the Church to those who had committed adultery or fornication, stated this was read in the church and pronounced in the church, and he designated this announcement as a promulgation.[8] But it is clear that what he designated as a promulgation was simply the public pronouncement of a decree already promulgated in Rome.

In 314 the Council of Arles sent to Pope Sylvester I (314-335) a letter in which was expressed the Council's regret that the pope had been unable to attend the sessions. The letter informed the pope regarding the enacted conciliar legislation, and at the same time asked him to publish the decrees of the Council

---

6 *De Pudicitia*, c. 1—*MPL*, II, 981.

7 Amann, "Penitence,"—*Dictionnaire de Theologie Catholique* (14 vols. in 23, Paris, 1903-1939), XII, 789.

8 *De Pudicitia*, c. 1: "Pontifex scilicet maximus, quod est Episcopus Episcoporum, edicit: 'Ego et moechiae et fornicationis delicta poenitentia functis dimitto.' O edictum, cui adscribi non poterit; 'Bonum factum!' Et ubi proponitur liberalitas ista? Ibidem opinor in ipsis libidinum januis, sub ipsis libidinum titulis. Illic ejusmodi poenitentia promulganda, ubi deliquentia ipsa versabitur; illic legenda est venia, quo cum spe ejus intrabitur. Sed hoc in ecclesia legitur, et in ecclesia pronuntiatur, et virgo est."—*MPL*, II, 981.

throughout his province.[9] Pope Siricius (384-399) in 385 wrote to Himerius, the Bishop of Tarragona, concerning various questions. He concluded his letter with the instruction that Himerius was to see to it that all the other bishops in his region became informed of the letter, not only those in his own diocese, but also those of the neighboring provinces.[10] In 415 Pope Innocent I (402-417) wrote to Alexander, the Bishop of Antioch, who had recently returned to the apostolic communion, concerning the treatment of the Arian clergy in Antioch. The letter ended with the instruction that its content was to be brought to the knowledge of all the bishops of the patriarchate, either by means of a synod, or through the public reading of the letter.[11]

Mention of the promulgation of papal law in Roman synods is found in a letter of Pope Hilarius (462) to the bishops of the provinces of France. He had sent to them the decrees promulgated by him that same year in Rome.[12] Again, in 488 Pope Felix III (483-492) sent to the clergy of Constantinople and Bithynia certain decrees on clerical discipline which he had promulgated previously in synod.[13]

That there were cases of extraordinary types of promulgation is shown from the letter of the Emperor Marcian (450-457) to Pope Leo the Great (440-461) in 453:

> "Miramur supra modum quod post Chalcedonensem Synodum, et litteras venerabilium Episcoporum ad tuam Sanctitatem missas, quibus omnia in ipsa synodo acta significabant, nullo prorsus pacto, a tua clementia ejusmodi epistolae remissae sint, quas videlicet in sanctissimis Ecclesiis perlectas

---

9 Mansi, *Sacrorum Conciliorum Nova et Amplissima Collectio* (53 vols. in 60, Parisiis, 1901-1927), II, 469: "Placuit etiam a te qui majores dioeceses tenes per te potissimum omnibus insinuari." (hereafter cited as Mansi).

10 "Haec quae ad tua rescripsimus consulta, in omnium coepiscoporum nostrorum perferri facias notionem, et non solum eorum qui in tua sunt dioecesi constituti, sed etiam ad universos Carthaginenses, ac Boeticos, Lusitanos atque Gallicos, vel eos qui vicinis tibi collimitant hinc inde provinciis, haec quae a nobis sunt salubri ordinatione disposita, sub litterarum tuarum prosecutione mittantur."—Mansi, III, 365; Jaffé, *Regesta Pontificum Romanorum ab condita Ecclesia ad annum post Christum natum MCXCVIII* (editionem 2. correctam et auctam auspiciis Gulielmi Wattenbach, curaverunt F. Kaltenbrunner, P. Ewald, S. Loewenfeld, 2 vols. in 1, Lipsiae, 1885-1888), n. 255 (work cited hereafter as JK for documents up to 590, as JE for the documents from 591 to 882, and as JL for the documents from 883 to 1198).

11 JK, n. 310; Mansi, III, 1056.

12 JK, n. 555; Mansi, VII, 934.

13 JK, n. 608; Mansi, VII, 1068.

> in omnium oportet notitiam pervenire. . . . Et ob eam rem tua pietas litteras mittere dignabitur, per quas omnibus Ecclesiis et populis manifestum fiat in sancta Synodo peracta, a tua Beatitudine rata haberi."[14]

The letter of the emperor showed that it was not unknown that laws should be published by means of a public reading in all the churches. The emperor mentioned that method as though it were quite customary.

Van Espen (1648-1728), in using as a basis for his argument some of these cited texts, stated that it was clear from the practice in that early period that the popes and the councils did realize the necessity of promulgating their laws in each province and diocese of the Christian world.[15] But a careful study of these texts reveals that such a conclusion does not necessarily follow, for, although the popes did send their letters and the decrees of the councils to the bishops of the various dioceses, it seems rather that such acts were more often the publication of a law which was already promulgated, either at Rome, or at the synod which issued the decree. The fact that the Church often did follow the method invoked by the civil law when there existed no method prescribed by ecclesiastical law does not prove that the Church was or considered itself bound to follow that law.

---

[14] Mansi, VI, 215.

[15] Van Espen, *Tractatus de Promulgatione Legum Ecclesiasticarum*, Pars I, c. III, §1 —*Scripta Omnia*, IV, 128.

Chapter II

The Promulgation of Law from 538 until the Time of Gratian

Article 1

Justinian's Novella 66

In the eleventh year of his reign (538) Justinian issued the first law that established a prescribed method of promulgation. This law is contained in his sixty-sixth Novella, *"Ut Factae Novae Constitutiones,"* and was originally, of course, meant to apply simply in the realm of civil laws. The subject of the imperial constitution was the form and the content of last wills and testaments. The writing of the constitution was occasioned by the fact that it had come to the knowledge of Justinian that statutes which he had previously enacted concerning wills were not known in the provinces, and at times not even in the city of Constantinople.

Justinian decreed that a copy of all laws concerning last wills should be sent to the provinces where the individual governors were to see to the promulgation of the laws by sending them to the individual cities of the province to be published, so that all the people could know of the new laws. To give everyone time to learn the law, the law did not begin to bind until two months after it had been promulgated in the province.[1] Thus the law did not begin to bind at the same time everywhere; the time varied in the provinces according to the particular time at which the law was promulgated in each province.

In the edition of the *Authenticum* which is accompanied with the *glossa*[2] this summary, as written by Angelus de Ubaldis (14th cent.), appears before the chapter: "Lex post insinua-

[1] N. (66.1): "Sed ut res etiam certius declaretur, sancimus si scribatur talis lex, ut illa post menses duos temporis ei dati valeat et in usu sit sive in hac felici urbe sive in provinciis, cum post insinuationem hoc tempus sufficiat ad eam omnibus manifestam reddendam, ut et tabelliones vim eius cognoscant et subditi eandem intellegant legemque servent."

[2] *Auth. Coll.*, V, tit. xvi.

tionem ligat in civitate Constantinopolitana; in provinciis vero post duos menses a die publicationis." From the text of the Novella one can note that this was not an accurate interpretation, since for the same period of two months the law remained inoperative also in the city of Constantinople. No indication was given by the canonical authors that the *vacatio legis* did not hold for the imperial city.

In the consideration of Novella 66, the first question that presents itself is whether this rule for the promulgation of laws applied only to testamentary legislation, or extended also to other laws. In the *Glossa ordinaria* Accursius (1185-1260) answered the latter part of the question thus: "Dico quod sic: ut patet ex rub. in princ. cuius verba sunt generalia; et ita hoc intelligi generaliter."[3] He gave two arguments. First, he argued from the general wording of the title of this Novella: "*Ut novae quae fiunt constitutiones postquam insinuatae sunt post duos menses alios valeant.*" The glossators established the general rule that the title of a constitution furnished an aid for the interpretation of the text as long as the title did not contradict the text. In this case, then, the title extended the application of the law. The argument "*a rubro ad nigrum*" was valid if the rubics were authentic, that is, if they were written by the lawmaker or were approved by him and if the rubrics contained a rule of law, and not simply an indication of the topic. So, since the rubrics of the Decretals of Gregory IX were authentic and those of Gratian were not, the argument "*a rubro ad nigrum*" could be used in the first case but not in the second. This held even if the rubrics extended the law.[4] In the case of the Novellae the rubrics were authentic, and hence they could extend the law.[5]

Secondly, the law regarding promulgation was generally accepted as holding not only for testimentary legislation, but for all imperial laws. Sometimes the emperor expressly excepted an individual law from this general enactment even when the law in question did not pertain to wills, e.g., in Novella 116,

---

[3] *Auth. Coll.*, V, tit. xvi. 1, *Glossa ordinaria*, s.v. *Huiusmodi legis.*

[4] Reiffenstuel, *Jus Canonicum Universum* (5 vols. in 7, Parisiis, 1864-1870), I, Proemium, n. 100.

[5] Reiffenstuel, *Jus Canonicum Universum*, I, Proemium, n. 111.

where the period of inoperative application of the law was restricted to thirty days. The fact that the emperor thought it necessary to make an express exception shows that he expected the law of Novella 66 to be followed in the publishing of every law, unless he made an express exception, even if the law did not pertain to last wills and testaments.

Now, in the empire of the sixth century the Church and State were so closely associated that the emperor often took it upon himself to legislate in ecclesiastical matters. When he did this, he prescribed the method of promulgation used for civil laws, namely, of promulgating the law in all the provinces, but he ordered this to be carried out through the hierarchy rather than through the civil officers.[6] In Novella 131, issued in the year 545, the regulations of the first four general councils were made a part of the civil law. For the first time they were officially promulgated as imperial law. The Novella was addressed, not to the patriarch, but to the praetorian prefect, and so it constituted general civil law. The emperor stated that he would provide for its promulgation in the provinces without cost to the taxpayers. So it is clear that much ecclesiastical legislation fell under Justinian's law regarding promulgation, namely all of that which the emperor himself enacted or which, when it had been previously enacted by ecclesiastical authorities, he incorporated into civil the law of the empire.

Article 2
Papal Legislation

As far as papal legislation was concerned, small in extent as it was, it appears that the publishing of Justinian's Novella 66 had little if any effect on the promulgation of papal law at that time. Even before the year 538 the popes were very careful that their laws should reach all those for whom they were meant, but there is no indication that after the new enactment of Justinian concerning promulgation the popes considered themselves likewise bound to promulgate their laws in all the provinces. Certainly no pope or council prescribed that all general

[6] N. 123, in which he prescribed the same method as was prescribed previously in Novella 5; cf. supra, p. 58.

ecclesiastical legislation had to be promulgated in all the provinces.

Examples of papal letters for this period show that the popes did not vary their practice of the previous centuries. In the year 545 Pope Vigilius (538-555) wrote to Auxanius, the Bishop of Arles, appointing him a papal vicar. The pope concluded the letter with the words: "Ea vero quae de praesenti ordinatione nostra directa praeceptione signavimus, ad universos episcopos per caritatem tuam volumus pervenire."[7]

In 683 Pope Leo II (682-683) sent to the bishops of Spain the acts of the VI Ecumenical Council, the III General Council of Constantinople, held in 680-681. In his letter he exhorted them to make known these definitions of the Council to their subjects.[8] So the papal constitutions and decretal letters of this period were still promulgated according to the methods used during the period before Justinian's Novella 66. Letters were sent by messenger to the bishops for whom they were meant, with instructions that they see to the publication of such laws in their own territory. At times the addressed bishops were instructed to make known the contents of the letter to the neighboring bishops. At other times the laws were to be promulgated in synod. These methods of promulgating papal legislation remained in common use until they were later replaced by the method introduced by Pope Martin IV (1281-1285), namely, of posting the new legislation in public places.

The period between the sixth and eleventh century was marked by a lack of formally general papal legislation. The decrees of the Eastern ecumenical councils together with those of the provincial councils in the West were gathered into collections on the private authority of canonists or of local ecclesiastical authorities, but none of these collections ever was approved by the Holy See as universal legislation for the Church. These private collections were passed from one diocese to another, copied and adopted by the various dioceses, and then had local or provincial legislation added to them.

---

[7] JK, n. 913; Mansi, IX, 41.

[8] "Ut per universos vestrae provinciae Praesules, sacerdotes et plebes, per religiosum vestrum studium innotescat, ac salubriter divulgetur."—Mansi, XI, 1052.

To these canons was added also the law as given in papal decretals. This papal legislation as contained in the decretal letters was not formal universal legislation, but rather a series of particular enactments, since it was given in the form of answers to problems proposed by individual bishops, or in *motu proprio* issued letters which were sent to a particular section of the Christian world. The period from the sixth to the ninth century was a period of national isolation in contrast to the unity of the empire. Rome lost control over the national churches, partly because the nations exercised individual control, and partly because the means of communication were diminished. The period was one of poverty in the development of canon law in Rome, and hence there was scarcely any problem concerning the promulgation of pontifical legislation for the universal Church.

This was the period when letters were marked with the notation "*a pari.*" When a papal letter was to be sent out to a number of bishops, one copy was retained in the chancery and was marked with the notation *a pari* or *a paribus* after the superscription in order to show that this same letter had been sent to more than one ordinary, somewhat in the manner of a modern encyclical letter. Letters bearing this notation, but dated back to a time before Pope Hormisdas in 519 have now been proven to be spurious.[9] This method of publishing papal legislation was used primarily not so much for promulgating new papal legislation, but rather for divulging that which had been previously promulgated. The purpose of sending identical letters from Rome was this, namely, to avoid the mistakes which inadvertently were made when a letter received by one bishop was copied and sent to another. An example of this type of letter is had in the letter written by Pope Hormisdas in 519, which was addressed, "Hormisdas Theodosio archidiacono Constantinopolitano et universis Catholicis a pari,"[10] and in the letter of John VIII in 882, the superscription of which read, "Richardi augustae seu Liutuuardo Vercellensi episcopo a paribus."[11]

[9] Silva-Tarouca, "Nouvi studi sulle antiche lettere dei papi,"—*Gregorianum,* XII (1939), 385.

[10] JK, n. 809; Mansi, VIII, 447.

[11] Mansi, XVII, 218.

Chapter III

The Promulgation of Law from the Time of Gratian until 1281

Before the time of Gratian the collections of law consisted mainly of the canons enacted in synods and councils; after his time the collections contained for the greater part the decretal letters directed by the popes to the bishops throughout the then known world. From the middle of the twelfth century a transformation in the manner of establishing canonical legislation took place. Until then synods and councils had played the important part in papal legislation, the popes preferring to legislate through these legal agencies. With a more generally manifested recognition of the universal papal authority, the decretal letters of the popes became important elements in the shaping of the Church's law. The change, begun under Pope Hadrian IV (1054-1059), was fully developed under Alexander III (1159-1181). Canonists came gradually to regard the papal decretals, though originally they had applied to individual cases, as sources of the Church's universal law, inasmuch as they accepted the principles and decisions given in decretal letters as having a binding force for the universal Church.

The post-Gratian period was the age of the glossators. These men contributed notably in the development of canonical jurisprudence. They wielded a powerful influence in shaping the law of the period, for their opinions were highly respected and their commentaries were frequently accepted as having the force of law in court. Because of the high esteem in which these men were held, there ensued the use of a new method for the promulgation of papal law.

In the year 1210 Pope Innocent III (1198-1216) formally approved the *Compilatio Tertia* which had been composed by Petrus Collivaccinus of Benevento. This approval gave rise to the first authentic collection of papal law in the history of the

Church. Along with the approval given to this compilation there was established a new method for the promulgation of ecclesiastical law. In the Bull "*Devotioni Vestrae*,"[1] addressed to the masters and scholars of the University of Bologna, the pope stated that this new compilation was sent to them so that without scruple they might use it both in the conducting of trials and in the teaching of law in the schools.

The *Compilatio Quinta*, probably composed by Tancred (†1235) and also an authentic collection, was promulgated in the same way as the *Compilatio Tertia*—by being sent to the University of Bologna. This was done by Honorius III on May 2, 1226, with the Bull "*Novae Causarum*."[2]

But far more important than the promulgation of these two compilations was that of the *Compilatio Decretalium D. Gregorii Papae IX*. The work of compiling was done by Saint Raymond of Peñafort (†1275) under the direction of the pope, who promulgated this new collection with the Bull "*Rex Pacificus*"[3] on September 5, 1234. It, too, was sent to the University of Bologna, and also to other universities, as for example those of Paris and of Padua.

During the next one hundred years seven other compilations were promulgated by being sent to the universities:

1. Innocent IV (1243-1254) was responsible for three collections, the first being a collection of twenty-two constitutions of the I General Council of Lyons (1245). He ordered these constitutions to be inserted in their proper places in the Decretals of Gregory IX, but despite this they were usually added as an appendix. This collection was sent to the University of Bologna with the Bull "*Cum nuper*"[4] on August 25, 1245.

2. On April 21, 1246, Innocent IV sent a second collection of eleven decretals to the Universities of Bologna and Paris with the Bull "*Cum inter venerabiles*."

---

[1] Augustinus, *Antiquae Collectiones Decretalium Commentariis et Emendationibus Illustratae*, F. 125.

[2] Cironius, *Opera in Jus Canonicum: Quinta Compilatio Epistolarum Honorii III, Pont. Max.* (Tolosae, 1645), p. 1.

[3] Potthast, n. 9694; bulla "*Rex Pacificus*" in pr. ad *Decretalium D. Gregorii Papae IX Compilatio, Corpus Iuris Canonici* (ed. Lipsien. 2., post Aemilii Ludovici Richteri curas instruxit Aemilius Friedberg, 2 vols., Lipsiae: Ex Officina Bernhardi, Tauchnitz, 1879-1881. Editio anastatice repetita, Lipsiae: Tauchnitz, 1922).

[4] Mansi, XXIII, 651.

3. Finally, combining these first two collections with eight more decretals, the same pope made a third collection consisting of forty-one officially promulgated decretals and constitutions. This collection was sent to the professors and students of Bologna by means of the Bull "*Ad explicandos*", on September 9, 1253.

4. The next collection was a compilation of the legislation of the II General Council of Lyons (1274) sent by Gregory X (1271-1276) on November 1, 1274, with the Bull "*Cum nuper*", to the Universities of Bologna, Paris and Pavia.

5. A small collection of five decretals was sent by Nicholas III (1277-1280) on March 23, 1280, to the University of Paris with the Bull "*Cum quasdam constitutiones.*"

6. Pope Boniface VIII (1294-1303) decided to collect all the legislation since the Decretals of Gregory IX into one collection which was to be a supplement to these Decretals. This *Liber Sextus* was published on March 3, 1298, with the Bull "*Sacrosanctae,*"[5] addressed to the doctors and students living at Bologna.

7. The Clementine Constitutions in the main were not decretals but rather statutes of Pope Clement V (1305-1314), especially those promulgated in the Council of Vienne (1311-1312). On March 21, 1314, he promulgated them in a consistory stating that they would have legal force as soon as they were sent to the schools. The pope died before they were sent, and they finally were sent out by his successor, Pope John XXII (1316-1334), with the Bull "*Quoniam nulla,*"[6] to the Universities of Bologna and Paris, on October 25, 1317.

Two other collections were later added to the *Corpus Iuris Canonici*, but they had not been promulgated as the previous collections. These added collections were the *Extravagantes* of John XXII and the *Extravagantes Communes.* The former collection contained twenty constitutions of Pope John XXII. The latter collection incorporated 33 constitutions of Pope John XXII (1316-1334), 11 of Pope Boniface VIII (1294-1303), 6 apiece of Popes Benedict XI (1303-1304), Clement V (1305-1314) and Sixtus IV (1471-1484), 4 of Pope Paul II (1464-1471), 2 of Pope Benedict XII (1334-1342), and 1 apiece of Popes Martin IV (1281-1285),

[5] *Corpus Iuris Canonici*, Friedberg ed., in pr. *Liber Sextus.*

[6] *Corpus Iuris Canonici*, Friedberg ed., in pr. *Constitutiones Clementinae.*

Clement VI (1342-1352), Urban V (1362-1370), Martin V (1417-1431), Eugene IV (1431-1447) and Calixtus III (1455-1458), for a total of 74 papal constitutions. Of this number four had already been incorporated in earlier collections.[7]

The practice then was not the same as it is in the present, when the enacted papal legislation is immediately promulgated to the universal Church. The laws contained in these collections usually were not new at the time when they were promulgated by being sent to the schools. It was the collections which were new, the laws having been issued at various times previous to the forming of the collections. In the case of the Decretals of Gregory IX many of the laws contained therein had been promulgated in synod or council previously; others were particular laws which had been derived from the earlier legislation of local synods, or also of papal decretals, and some were even derived from spurious texts which had been invented by the forgers. All of these, once they were included in the Decretal collection, were formally promulgated by Gregory IX and were given thereby the force of universal ecclesiastical law. Thus certain spurious legislation became authentic, certain particular laws became universal, and by their simultaneous promulgation the laws which had been issued at various times all became binding for the universal Church at one and the same time.

With the later collections, too, even though the legislation contained in them had often already been promulgated, as for example the constitutions drawn up in the two General Councils of Lyons, their transmision to the universities was not always merely a case of the publication of a law already promulgated. That, indeed, was sometimes the case, as in the example just mentioned; on the other hand, particular papal decretals when included in these collections obtained the force of universal legis-

[7] The Constitution *Super cathedram* of Boniface VIII (Feb. 18, 1300) had appeared in the Clementine Collection (c.2, *de sepulturis*, III, 6 in Extravag. com. = c. 2, *de sepulturis*, III, 7 in Clem.), and the Constitutions *Suscepti regiminis* (Oct. 25, 1317) (c. un., *ne sede vacante aliquid innovetur*, II, 3, in Extravag. com. = c. 2, *de electione et electi potestate*, tit. I, Extravag. Joan. XXII), *Sedes apostolica* (Oct. 30, 1317) (c. un., *de officio delegati*, I, 6, in Extravag. com. = c. un., *de concessione praebendae et ecclesiae non vacantis*, tit. IV, in Extravag. Joan. XXII) and *Exsecrabiles quorundam* (Nov. 19, 1317) (c. 4, *de praebendis et dignitatibus*, III, 2, in Extravag. com. = c. un., *de praebendis et dignitatibus*, tit. III, in Extravag. Joan. XXII) of John XXII had appeared earlier also in this pope's collection which contained 20 of his constitutions.

lation through their formal promulgation in connection with the collection which contained them. Before this act of promulgation the individual papal decretals were indeed considered as law, but they formally existed as particular law enacted in answer to the query of an individual bishop or metropolitan, or they formally represented an instruction to some bishop or to a group of bishops in a particular section of the world. Such decretals, then, were not promulgated to the universal Church before their inclusion in these collections. The same was true of those constitutions which later were never incorporated in the collections. They did have a legal force, and they were indeed promulgated, but not as part of a collection. Their promulgation was effected according to the methods in general use at the time they were issued.

The promulgation of laws by means of sending collections of them to the universities was, therefore, not the only method used for the promulgation of papal laws during the period here discussed. The old methods, as described in the previous chapter, were still used when there was question of particular legislation enacted through the issuing of constitutions and decretals; it was simply with reference to the recounted ten authentic collections that the act of promulgation consisted in the fact that they had been sent to the universities for use and application in the courts and in the schools.

Lijdsman states that there was another collection promulgated by means of being sent to the University of Bologna. Pope Benedict XIV made a collection of the constitutions, encyclical letters, etc. issued by him during the first six years of his pontificate, and he sent the collection to the University of Bologna with the Constitution *Jam fere sextus*. Lijdsman claims that this amounted to a promulgation of the collection.[8]

No other author mentions this collection as an example of the method of promulgation by means of the sending of a collection of laws to the universities. And Lijdsman does not attempt to prove that what he says is correct. It is not at all certain that this can be called a promulgation of the collection. The pope did not say in the letter *Jam fere sextus* that he was promulgating his collection. Furthermore, in the letter the pope indicates that the

[8] *Introductio in Jus Canonicum*, p. 377.

reason he made the collection was to save posterity the trouble of collecting his acts later on. He seems to have sent the collection to the university as a favor to them and because the men there were the ones who would make best use of it. Finally, the pope says that almost everything contained in the collection has already been made public; documents pertaining to private affairs were omitted. Hence, there was no need for promulgating the collection, since its contents had already been promulgated by him.

It seems, therefore, that the pope sent this collection to the University of Bologna not in order to promulgate it but rather as a favor to the university to show that he was dedicating the work to the professors and students there.

CHAPTER IV

The Promulgation of Papal Legislation from 1281 until 1908

ARTICLE 1

Ordinary Methods of Promulgation

Since there was no legislation to determine the way in which universal ecclesiastical laws were to be published, no one fixed method of promulgation was used exclusively in the Church. During the fourteenth and fifteenth centuries several ways for the promulgation of papal legislation were in use. In the previous chapter consideration was given to the method used by a number of the popes in promulgating their laws by sending a compilation of the laws to the universities. At the same time the older method of promulgation in synod was retained. Much of the legislation of the Western Ecumenical Councils, from the I General Council of the Lateran (1123) to the General Council of Constance (1414–1418), consisted of papal constitutions which were promulgated before the assembled Council.

There was, however, still a third method of promulgation in use at that time, and it became the one most commonly used in the Church from the fifteenth until the twentieth century. Authors commonly hold that this method of promulgation was introduced by Pope Martin IV (1281–1285) in the year 1281,[1] when he caused copies of the Bull "*Michaelem,*"[2] in which he excommunicated the Emperor Michael VIII Palaeologus (1259–1282), to be attached to the doors of the papal residence in Orvieto. In this bull the pope

[1] Zaccaria, *De Rebus ad Historiam atque Antiquitates Ecclesiae Pertinentibus Dissertationes Latinae* (4 vols., Fulginiae, 1781), Dissertatio XI, Vol. II, 206 (hereafter cited as *Dissertationes*); Bouix, *De Principiis*, p. 247; Michiels, *Normae Generales Juris Canonici*, I, 235; Cicognani, *Canon Law*, p. 552; Maroto, *Institutiones Iuris Canonici*, I, 197; Van Hove, *De Legibus*, p. 136; Creagh, "The Promulgation of Pontifical Law,"—*The Catholic University Bulletin*, XV (1909), 29.

[2] Potthast, n. 21815; *Bullarium*, IV, 52; Mansi, XXIV, 105.

clearly indicated that this method of publication was sufficient to make the sentence known to the universal Church, and hence by this act of publication the bull was officially promulgated. It is true that this bull implied a sentence of excommunication and not the enactment of a law, but the method of promulgation introduced by this decree was used also for the promulgation of laws from that time onward.

Van Espen (1648–1728) stated that this method of promulgation was nowhere mentioned in the books of the *Corpus Iuris Canonici.*[3] That statement of course is true. But his conclusion that therefore this method of promulgation was unknown before the time of Pope John XXII (1316–1334) does not follow. Certainly laws were posted in the public places as early as 1282, and a sentence of excommunication was similarly posted in 1281. It is possible that even before that time this same method of promulgation was used. Zaccaria (1714–1795) stated that he suspected very much that even before the time of Martin IV the same method was used by Innocent IV (1243–1254), when he excommunicated Ezzelino IV (1194–1259),[4] but there is nothing in the bull to indicate that this was the case.[5] This method of promulgation was first used for the publishing of universal law by Martin IV in the year 1282, when in his Bull "*Cogit nos temporis,*"[6] which enacted an excommunication for all who gave aid to the Saracens in Sicily, he ordered that the law be attached to the doors of the papal palace in Orvieto.

In many bulls, and especially in those containing universal legislation, the popes after 1282 gave directions as to the manner of the promulgation of the laws enacted by them. The formula used was almost the same in every case. Although there were slight variations in the form, the content was usually the same. The formula most often found is the one which was first used by Pope Martin IV in the Bull "*Michaelem,*" or one almost the same: "Ut autem praesentes litterae ad omnium notitiam deducantur, volumus et mandamus illas in valvis . . . affigi et publicari, ut ii, quos

---

[3] *De Promulgatione Legum Ecclesiasticarum,* Pars I, c. III, §7—*Scripta Omnia,* IV, 131.

[4] *Dissertationes,* II, 227.

[5] *Bullarium,* III, 586.

[6] Potthast, n. 21895; Mansi, XXIV, 391.

litterae ipsae concernunt, quod ad ipsos non pervenerint, aut illos ignoraverint nullam possint excusationem praetendere vel ignorantiam allegare, cum non sit verisimile quod ad ipsos remaneat incognitum quod tam patenter fuerit publicatum."

Another formula frequently found is the one used by Pope Sixtus IV (1471–1484) in his Bull "*Romanus Pontifex*" of August 10, 1478.[7] There were slight variations in the terminology of this formula, but the most frequent form of this formula in later times was the one which was employed in the Bull "*Pastoralis Officii*" of Pope Pius IV, on April 3, 1560:[8] "Volumus autem quod cum primum praesentes literae, quorum transumptis, manu notarii publici subscriptis, sicuti ipsis originalibus literis, fidem plenam adhiberi debere decernimus, in valvis basilicae Principis Apostolorum de Urbe et ecclesiae Lateranensis ac acie Campi Florae etiam de Urbe per unum ex cursoribus nostris affixae fuerint, perinde singulos, quos concernunt, quoad praemissa omnia arctent, ac si eaedem praesentes literae eis singulariter et personaliter insinuatae et intimatae fuissent."

In many other instances, even though the Sovereign Pontiff did not give instructions in the bull itself as to the method of promulgation to be used, there has been added to the bull a record of the publication as made by the *cursores*. From these records one can determine how, when and where the papal constitutions were published.

The places in which the laws were published were usually the same. In Rome almost always they were affixed to the doors of the Basilica of Saint Peter, and very frequently also to those of the Lateran Basilica, of the Apostolic Chancery and in the public square known as the Campo di Fiori. At times other places also were prescribed, but rather by way of exception. From the following list the reader can gain an idea of the places where the laws were posted.

Sept. 3, 1299, "*Fuit olim*" of Boniface VIII—St. John Lateran;[9]
March 30, 1317, "*Si Fratrum*" of John XXII—Church at Avignon;[10]

---

[7] *Bullarium*, V, 266.
[8] *Bullarium*, VII, 18.
[9] *Bullarium*, IV, 152.
[10] *Bullarium*, IV, 234.

Oct. 27, 1375, "*Solicite vitari*" of Gregory XI—Avignon;[11]
Sept. 18, 1390, "*Caeca cupiditas*" of Boniface IX—St. Peter's;[12]
Nov. 17, 1461, "*Cum ex sacrorum*" of Pius II—Apostolic Chancery;[13]
Aug. 10, 1478, "*Romanus Pontifex*" of Sixtus IV—St. Peter's and S. Maria ad Martyres;[14]
Aug. 23, 1485, "*Cum ab Apostolica*" of Innocent VIII—Apostolic Chancery;[15]
Jan. 25, 1491, "*Officii Nostri*" of Innocent VIII—Apostolic Chancery;[16]
The Bull "*Cum ex relatione*" of Alexander VI published in St. Peter's on Dec. 24 and 25, 1497, and in the Apostolic Chancery and the Campo di Fiori on Jan. 13, 1498;[17]
Nov. 27, 1505, "*Cum homines*" of Julius II—St. Peter's and St. John Lateran;[18]
Dec. 13, 1507, "*Apostolatus officium*" of Julius II—Apostolic Chancery, Campo di Fiori, Papal residence;[19]
June 1, 1741, "*Sacramentum Poenitentiae*" of Benedict XIV—St. John Lateran, St. Peter's, Apostolic Chancery, General Curia in Monte Citatorio, Campo di Fiori;[20]
Sept. 3, 1746, "*Ad universae christianae*" of Benedict XIV—St. Peter's, Apostolic Chancery, Campo di Fiori.[21]

Towards the end of the fourteenth century there was added to this method of promulgation by means of posting the copies of the text in the aforementioned places a public reading of the bull at a time when a large congregation had gathered. Immediately after this reading by the *cursores* the text was taken by the same men and attached to the doors of the place in which it had been read. There are evidences of papal bulls promulgated in this way as early as 1375, when on October 27 of that year Pope

[11] *Bullarium*, IV, 577.
[12] *Bullarium*, IV, 604.
[13] *Bullarium*, V, 165.
[14] *Bullarium*, V, 266.
[15] *Bullarium*, V, 316.
[16] *Bullarium*, V, 346.
[17] *Bullarium*, V, 369.
[18] *Bullarium*, V, 415.
[19] *Bullarium*, V, 465.
[20] *Benedicti XIV, Pont. Opt. Max. olim Prosper Cardinalis De Lambertinis Bullarium* (3 vols. in 4, Prati, 1845-1847), I, 65 (hereafter cited as *Bullarium Benedicti XIV*).
[21] *Bullarium Benedicti XIV*, II, 121.

Gregory XI issued his Bull "*Solicite vitari*," which was read in a public audience.[22]

Later on this method became very common, and almost all of the constitutions which were posted in the usual places were first read before they were posted. The Bull "*Romanus Pontifex*," issued by Sixtus IV on August 10, 1478, was read publicly before the copies were attached to the doors of Saint Peter's. At the conclusion of the Bull "*Cum ab Apostolica Sede*," issued by Innocent VIII on August 23, 1485, to revoke the concessions of the rights of patronage and of the presentation of candidates for benefices as granted during the twenty-five years previous, there is the following note concerning its publication: "Lecta in Camera Apostolica . . . "[23]

An example of a text prescribing a public reading is had in the Bull "*Inter graves*" of Pope Leo X, May 26, 1515. The promulgated law forbade the occupation of any papal lands or the invasion of places belonging to the Holy See:

> "Anno a nativitate Domini 1515, indictione tertia, die vero 26 maii, pontificatus sanctiss. in Christo patris et D.N.D. Leonis divina providentia Papae X, anno III, retroscriptae literae apostolociae, ut ad omnium notitiam citius deveniant, alto et intelligibili voce de verbo ad verbum lectae fuerunt in valvis basilicae Principis Apostolorum ac ecclesiae S. Joannis Lateranensis, dum ibidem divina celebrarentur et multitudo populi adesset; nec non earumdem ecclesiarum et Cancellariae Apostolicae valvis seu portis, ac acie Campi Florae affixae et publicatae . . . "[24]

From the fourteenth century, therefore, until the twentieth the most frequent method used for the promulgating of pontifical law was this method of attaching the copies of the text of the law in public places, and of reading them before large gatherings of the public. The public reading, however, was done in addition to the posting of the text of the law. The reading did not always accompany the posting. In more recent times the reading became less

[22] *Bullarium*, IV, 577.
[23] *Bullarium*, V, 316.
[24] *Bullarium*, V, 625.

common than it had been between the fifteenth and the eighteenth centuries.

In his Constitution *Promulgandi,* issued on September 29, 1908, Pope Pius X mentioned a method of promulgation which had become customary for a few decades preceding the issuance of this constitution. From the year 1870 it had become the practice that the laws of the Holy See, especially those issued through the various Congregations of the Roman Curia, were promulgated by means of a publication of the new law in the office of the Secretary of the Congregation which issued the law.[25]

Article 2

Extraordinary Methods of Promulgation

In modern times some of the most important utterances of the Holy See have been given in the form of encyclical letters. These letters in their present form date back to the time of the reign of Pope Benedict XIV (1740–1758), although the word has been applied to certain papal letters for many centuries. In the first year of his pontificate Pope Benedict XIV on December 3, 1740, issued a letter entitled "*Epistola Encyclica et Commonitorio ad omnes Episcopos,*" expounding the duties of bishops.[26] Among the later encyclicals are the: "*Quanta cura*" of Pius IX on December 8, 1864; "*Rerum novarum*" of Leo XIII, May 16, 1891; Pius X's "*Acerbo nimis,*" April 15, 1905, and "*Pascendi*" on September 8, 1907.

Cicognani states that encyclicals in which laws are established are rare, but he does admit that certain cases of encyclicals establishing new legislation have occurred, and he gives as examples the encyclicals of Pope Pius X, "*Acerbo nimis*" and "*Pascendi.*"[27] In the latter encyclical letter, which was written against Modernism, the Sovereign Pontiff made a number of regulations which

---

[25] *Acta Apostolicae Sedis, Commentarium Officiale* (Romae, 1909-), I (1909), 5. (hereafter cited *AAS*).

[26] "*Ubi Primum*"—*Benedicti XIV Bullarium,* I, 3; *Codicis Iuris Canonici Fontes, cura Emi Petri Card. Gasparri editi* (9 vols., Romae [postea Civitate Vaticana]: Typis Polyglottis Vaticanis, 1923-1939) (Vols. VII-IX, ed. cura et studio Emi Justiniani Card. Serédi), n. 304. (hereafter cited *Fontes*).

[27] *Canon Law,* p. 84.

bound the bishops to whom it was addressed. For example, they were ordered to furnish the Holy See with a diligently prepared sworn report concerning not only the fulfillment of the prescriptions contained in the encyclical, but also the doctrines that were current among the clergy, especially in the seminaries. This was to be done within a year after the publishing of the papal letter, and every three years thereafter.

Thus the encyclical letter represented an exceptional method of promulgating the laws of the Holy See. The text of the letter was not posted in the public places, as was usually done with newly enacted legislation before the year 1908, but rather the letter was sent to all the patriarchs, primates, archbishops and bishops and other local ordinaries in communion with the Apostolic See. Encyclical letters issued after 1908 were published in the official publication, the *Acta Apostolicae Sedis.*

There are other examples of exceptional ways used for the promulgating of papal legislation, and these methods were prescribed in the constitution of the popes. On August 4, 1487, Pope Innocent VIII in the Constitution *Etsi ex iniuncto nobis,*[28] which condemned some heretical propositions of Giovanni Pico de Mirandola (1463–1494) and prohibited the reading and the publishing of them, ordered that this letter be published in the churches of the cities of his diocese by each ordinary to whom it was sent.

Pope Julius II on March 1, 1511, in his Constitution *Consueverunt Romini Pontifices,*[29] issued by him as a *Bulla in Coena Domini* which listed the currently enacted penalties, ordered it to be posted in Rome, as usual, on the doors of the churches of St. Peter and St. John Lateran, but commanded besides that it was to be read once or even oftener every year, throughout the world in all the churches. Of course, the repeated reading in this case did not constitute a promulgation of the law, but implied rather a new publication of the promulgated law.

In his Constitution *Decet Romanum Pontificem,* Leo X on January 3, 1521, condemned the errors of Luther and his followers together with the doctrine that they taught. This bull was to

[28] *Bullarium,* V, 327.
[29] *Bullarium,* V, 491.

be promulgated by being posted on the doors of two cathedral or metropolitan churches in Germany.[30] On March 21, 1542, Pope Paul III in his Bull "*Cupientes Iudaeos,*" which explained the privileges of Jewish and infidel converts and established regulations concerning their way of life, ordered that it be published once a year in all cathedral and collegiate churches and in other pious places.[31]

The Constitution *Cum quorundam* of Paul IV on August 7, 1555, was posted in Rome in the usual places, and outside the city in the churches throughout the various dioceses.[32]

What amounted to a personal promulgation was required in the case of the bull which suppressed the Society of Jesus. The Brief "*Dominus ac Redemptor noster*" of Clement XIV, which was issued by him on July 21, 1773, was to achieve its binding effect in a house of the Order only if it was promulgated by special agents in that house.[33] On May 8, 1881, Pope Leo XIII issued his Constitution *Romanos Pontifices.* It effected a settlement of certain controversies which had arisen between the bishops of England and Scotland on the one hand and the regulars on the other who worked as missionaries in these countries. Copies of the letter were to be published, but the particular method of publication was left within the discretion of the bishops. It is evident that the Constitution was not to be considered as promulgated previously to its publication in England and Scotland, for it was plainly stated in the Constitution that its prescriptions were to become binding upon its publication in these countries.[34]

The Decree "*Ne temere,*" issued on August 2, 1907, was promulgated in an exceptional way when a copy of the decree was sent out to all local ordinaries throughout the world.[35]

---

30 *Bullarium,* V, 761.

31 *Bullarium,* VI, 336.

32 *Bullarium,* VI, 500.

33 *Bullarii Romani Continuatio Summorum Pontificum* (9 vols. in 12, Prati, (1835-1856) IV, 619. (hereafter cited as *Bullarii Continuatio*).

34 §30: "Quocumque autem modo earumdem praesentium Litterarum exempla in Anglia publicata fuerint, volumus ut statim post huiusmodi publicationem omnes et singulas quas concernunt vel concernent in posterum perinde afficiant, ac si unicuique illorum personaliter intimatae ac notificatae fuissent."—*Leonis XIII Pontificis Maximi Acta* (23 vols., Romae, 1881-1905), II, 231; *Fontes,* n. 582.

35 Wernz-Vidal, *Ius Canonicum,* I, 191, fnt. 83; Coronata, *Institutiones Iuris Canonici,* I, 20.

Article 3

Controversy Concerning the Necessity of Promulgating Universal Pontifical Legislation in Each Diocese

Before the issuance of the Constitution *Promulgandi* on September 29, 1908, there was a controversy among canonists concerning the juridical import of the promulgation effected by the posting of a copy of the law in the public places of the city of Rome. In earlier times a number of reputable canonists held that it was not sufficient for the promulgation of universal legislation that the law be published only in the city of Rome. Rather, they demanded that if the whole world was to be bound by a law, the whole world should be informed of the new law officially, and this could be accomplished only by the promulgation of the law in every province or diocese of the whole world.

This controversy was an old one, dating back to the time of the decretalists of the fourteenth century, and it continued in evidence until the time of Pope Pius X. The main argument advanced in favor of the need of a diocesan promulgation for universal legislation adverted to the supplementary character of the Roman Law in relation to the Canon Law. If a matter was not covered by the canons, it was to be decided according to the provisions of the Roman Law. When Pope Pius X issued the first canon law on the method which was to be used in the promulgating of ecclesiastical law, their argument was no longer valid, and thus the controversy about this question was ended. At the present time, then, there is no such controversy; the controversy is accordingly of a purely historical character.

A slight difference of terminology appears among the authors who denied that promulgation in Rome was sufficient to make a law binding throughout the world. They defended the necessity of a promulgation by means of a posting of the text of the law in each diocese, or in each province, or in each country. Substantially this implied no difference in their argumentation, for their real thesis was that promulgation in Rome alone was not sufficient; there had to be an official publication all through the world, and it mattered little whether this was to be made in each country, in each province, or in each diocese. For brevity's sake in the present discussion simply the term diocese will be used.

The difference of opinion among the authors was occasioned by two factors: 1) by the lack of any ecclesiastical legislation concerning the official manner of promulgating universal law, and 2) by the method that was in common use from 1281 until 1908, namely, of promulgating pontifical laws in the city of Rome alone. The discussion began soon after this method of promulgation was introduced by Pope Martin IV in 1281. The first opinion—that promulgation in Rome alone was not sufficient—enjoyed at first at least an extrinsic probability, for it had more than a few defenders of good canonical repute. It was, however, never the more common opinion. Sylvius (1581-1649) called this opinion probable, but he acknowledged that the opposite opinion—that promulgation in Rome alone was sufficient unless the pope signified otherwise in a particular instance—carried greater probability of correctness.[36]

In the course of time the less common opinion waned even more in favor because of the fact that, if the pope was forced to promulgate all his legislation in every diocese, it would make him dependent on the kings and even on the bishops who could prevent the promulgation in their territories. Suarez, in the early part of the seventeenth century, attested the fact that the theory which favored a publication in Rome as being sufficient was the more common doctrine,[37] and by the time of Saint Alphonsus Liguori (1696-1787) that doctrine could be called "*valde communis et probabilior.*"[38] It seems that after the middle of the eighteenth century the onetime less common opinion was not defended by any canonists of standing in the Church.

The main arguments advanced by those who held that a law had to be promulgated in every diocese in order to be binding in the Universal Church can be reduced to the following:[39]

36 *Commentarium in Summam Theologicam Sancti Thomae Aquinatis,* in I.II., q. 96, a. 4, quaer. xi, concl. 3.

37 *De Legibus,* Lib. IV, cap. xv, n. 3.

38 *Theologia Moralis,* Lib. I, n. 96.

39 Cf. Navarrus, *Opera Omnia* (6 vols., Venetiis, 1618), I, c. 23, n. 44; another who held this view was Van Espen, *Tractatus de Promulgatione Legum Ecclesiasticarum,* Pars. I, c. III—*Scripta Omnia,* IV, 128. Van Hove (*De Legibus,* p. 137) cites Petrus de Marca (†1662) and Febronius (†1790) as having held this opinion. Many authors cite Panormitanus as having favored this same view because of his statement in his

1. When there was no provision of canon law on a certain matter, then it was the will of the Church that the civil (Roman) law be followed, as long as the civil law prescribed nothing that militated against good morals or religion. This was proved: a) from the words of Pope Lucius III (1181-1185),[40] which indicated that if the canon law was silent then the civil law could be followed, b) and from the Decree of Gratian, which in one of its canons defended this principle in the following words: "Si in adiutorium vestrum terreni imperii leges assumendas putatis, non reprehendimus. Fecit hoc Paulus cum adversus iniuriosos Romanum civem se esse testatur."[41]

2. The popes sometimes did order that a law be promulgated in each diocese throughout the world. This indicated that whenever they intended to bind the whole world the popes provided for a promulgation by posting a copy of the law in each diocese. The defenders of this opinion likewise appealed to a text in the Decretals of Gregory IX in support of their doctrine. Innocent III had written: "Si quis autem medicorum huius nostrae constitutionis, postquam per praelatos locorum fuerit publicata, transgressor extiterit . . ." This text was part of canon 22 of the IV General Council of Lateran (1215). Since it explicitly presupposed that the law was to be published by every prelate, it implicitly pointed to the need of promulgation in each diocese.[42] Van Espen pointed to the established practice in the early history of the Church in support of the same contention.[43] If the popes in the early Church used the method of promulgating their laws in every diocese, then, so he stated, they must have recognized that method of promulgation as necessary for the establishment of a universally binding law.

3. The fact that in papal constitutions the Sovereign Pontiffs declared explicity that by its promulgation in Rome a law was just as binding as if it had been personally intimated to each

commentary on c. 2, X, *de constitutionibus*, I, 2, but he could also be cited for the opposite opinion, since in his commentary on c. 49, X, *de sententia excommunicationis*, V, 39, he evidently had changed his mind.

40 "Sicut leges non dedignantur sacros canones imitari, ita et sacrorum statuta canonum principum constitutionibus adiuvantur."—c. 1, X, *de novi operis nuntiatione*, V, 32.

41 C. 7, D. X.

42 C. 13, X, *de poenitentiis et remissionibus*, V, 38.

43 *Tractatus de Promulgatione Legum Ecclesiasticarum*, Pars. I, c. II, §2—*Scripta Omnia*, IV, 126.

individual was an indication that this was ordinarily not the case, for otherwise such an explicit mention would have served no useful purpose.

4. It would have been too harsh a burden on the faithful if the Church had bound everyone in the world to obey a law promulgated by publication in the city of Rome alone, for many Christian communities were far removed from this center. Even the law of Our Lord did not bind everywhere as soon as it was promulgated in Jerusalem on Pentecost Sunday. It bound only when it became sufficiently published throughout the world. Van Espen claimed that it was morally impossible for the people of all the dioceses throughout the world to obtain certain knowledge of a law which was published in Rome alone. If the law became known it was often only through vague rumors and private announcements, and such agencies did not suffice for the official promulgation of papal legislation to the community.[44]

5. It was universally recognized that a law had to be promulgated before it bound, and that promulgation consisted in an official publication of the law in such a way that the community could obtain knowledge of the law without great difficulty. This was a demand inherent in the nature of law itself. The manner in which the promulgation was effected remained immaterial, as long as it met this requirement of the natural law. An act of promulgation by publication exclusively in the city of Rome was not, however, an effective means for the promulgating of a universal law, since it proved insufficient to make the law known to the entire Catholic community. Therefore the natural law demanded the publication of the law in each diocese.

6. The very notion of ecclesiastical government as instituted by Christ required that the act of promulgation be effected in every diocese. Christ did not wish his Church to govern its subjects as a master dominates his slaves; rather, instead of constraint through fear of punishment, it was the attraction inspired by love and devotion that was to win obedience to the law of the Church. Therefore in the application of ecclesiastical legislation all that was clearly harsh or burdensome was to be sedu-

[44] *Tractatus de Promulgatione Legum Ecclesiasticarum*, Pars. I, c. III, §3—*Scripta Omnia*, IV, 129.

lously avoided by the heirarchy. Even the opponents of the doctrine here supported were in agreement that in the case of civil laws the civil rulers were bound to publish their laws in every province. If the same rule did not apply in the promulgation of ecclesiastical laws, then the following paradox would be inevitable: ecclesiastical authorities, who are supposed to rule paternally with love and regard for their subjects, would actually impose a harsher burden on the people than the emperors, who might well have been expected to have less regard for their subjects. Hence it appears necessary, if universal ecclesiastical legislation was to become binding, that it be promulgated in every diocese throughout the world.

By far the majority of canonists through the centuries have supported the theory that it was sufficient for the promulgation of a universal pontifical law that the law be promulgated in Rome only, so that a diocesan promulgation was not deemed necessary.[45]

1. The method of promulgation was a matter which depended on the will of the one who made the law. The popes in their constitutions expressed their will in this matter by stating explicitly that their laws bound everywhere, even though they were promulgated only in the city of Rome.

2. From the letter of Pope Innocent III to the cathedral chapter of the archdiocese of Sens[46] it was clear that the Holy Father considered all bound once they knew that the law had been solemnly promulgated, even though it had not been promulgated directly to them in their territory.

3. It was customary in the Church to consider the laws which had been promulgated in Rome as binding upon all the faithful. There were many rescripts, bulls and papal letters which were considered binding everywhere, even though they had never been promulgated outside Rome. An example of this was the *Bulla Coenae Domini.*

4. Inasmuch as the Church constituted one mystical body, it was very fitting that the laws which had been promulgated in

---

[45] For the arguments in favor of this opinion see: Reiffenstuel, *Jus Canonicum Universum*, Lib. I, tit. II, nn. 117 sqq.; Alphonsus Maria de Ligorio, *Theologia Moralis*, Lib. I, n. 96; Bouix, *De Principiis*, pp. 230 sqq.; Suarez, *De Legibus*, Lib. IV, cap. xv.

[46] C. 1, X, *de postulatione praelatorum*, I, 5.

the capital city should bind everywhere for the whole mystical body.[47]

Besides these positive arguments in favor of the more common opinion, the authors likewise furnished negative arguments in refutation of the view advanced by their opponents.

1. In answer to the first argument above presented by the minority opinion it can be stated that the principle which they upheld, namely, that when legislation was lacking in the law of the Church concerning a certain matter, then the Roman civil law provided a norm of action, was not denied by those authors who opposed them. On the contrary, the principle was generally followed. Yet, it was not considered essential to follow the civil law in such a case, since the civil law merely presented a usable norm. The popes certainly could deviate from the practice of the civil authorities by declaring that another method of promulgation be used in the promulgation of ecclesiastical legislation, and that is precisely what they did in the constitutions they issued.

2. It was not denied that often the popes did prescribe promulgation in each diocese, but to deduce from this that only then did they intend to bind the universal Church would be contrary to the facts of history. It was by way of exception that a promulgation in each diocese was ordered, as was done in the decree of the IV Lateran Council which they quoted. That the popes did intend to bind all the faithful by the laws which they promulgated at Rome was clear both from the wording of the text of the constitutions and from the fact that it was generally accepted that the universal Church was bound by these laws.

3. It was not because they recognized that promulgation in each diocese was necessary unless another method was explicitly provided that the popes stated in their constitutions that a promulgation at Rome sufficed. The reason for the expresss mention, in so many of the papal constitutions, of the fact that the law by publication in Rome alone bound everyone in the whole world was that some persons had questioned the legality of laws and sentences promulgated by publication of the law in Rome alone.

[47] Suarez, *De Legibus*, Lib. IV, cap. xv, n. 6.

4. The fact that many parts of the Catholic world were far removed from Rome did not imply that an exclusive promulgation of the law in the city of Rome would entail a discrimination against the faithful far distant, for Rome was the center of Christianity, and to that city came Christians from every part of the world who could easily carry back the notice of the newly promulgated papal laws. Many bishops had representatives at Rome to inform them of the acts of the Pontiffs. Another way in which the law quickly and without difficulty could be made known throughout the world was through the many apostolic legates to whom the popes sent news of the newly promulgated laws. So it was not morally impossible, as Van Espen stated, for the people to obtain certain knowledge of the laws promulgated in Rome. Bouix declared that the acquisition of this knowledge was not only possible but also very easy.[48] Furthermore, there was no question of any inequitable discrimination, for the law did not bind the subjects, at least as far as guilt and penalties were concerned, until they had received notice of the law.

5. It was always true that a law had to be presented by the lawmaker to the community in such a way that all the subjects could obtain knowledge of the law without great difficulty. But that did not mean that all had to come to a knowledge of the law at the same time, for even by a diocesan promulgation such a result could not be accomplished. Hence the fact that it required some time for those far from Rome to receive notice of a law promulgated there did not imply that such a promulgation militated against the demands of the natural law.

6. If it were a postulate of the natural law that all universal papal legislation be promulgated in every part of the world, then it would inexorably follow that for over six centuries the Church did not know, or else willfully violated, a part of the natural law. It would mean that throughout that period of time the popes erred when they asserted in their constitutions that by a law promulgated only in the city of Rome the whole Catholic world was bound. Such a conclusion is untenable.

7. It is not necessary here to discuss the nature of the government established by Christ for his Church. The present argu-

[48] *De Principiis*, p. 237.

ment centers solely upon the allegation that the Church put a harsher burden on her subjects than did the civil rulers on theirs, inasmuch as the civil rulers did promulgate their laws in every province of their realm. There was no undue discrimination against the people through the Church's method of the exclusive promulgation of her laws in Rome, for the subjects under the law were not considered bound *in actu secundo* by the laws until they knew of them. In practice there was no difference, as far as the people were concerned, between the promulgating of a law in a number of places on the one hand, and, on the other, the promulgating of it in only one place along with the subsequent sending of notice to the rest of the world.

From the arguments that have been presented it is readily seen that a posting of the text of an ecclesiastical law in various places in the city of Rome was constituted as a sufficient promulgation of the law. By such promulgation the law was instituted as a universal ecclesiastical law, and it began to bind *in actu secundo* all those subject to the Holy See who knew about it. Probably the most foreceful argument in favor of this opinion was that which appealed to the intention of the Roman Pontiffs. Since the method of the promulgation of a law depends on the will of the superior who makes the law, it was the right of the popes to choose any adequate means of promulgating universal ecclesiastical laws. In article 2 of this chapter the formulae used in the papal constitutions in prescribing the means of promulgation were discussed. From a study of the wording of these formulae it is clear that the popes did wish to bind all the faithful by their laws independently of their promulgation in the dioceses. And it was certainly in this way that the great majority of canonists interpreted the words which the popes used in the formulae attached to their constitutions. Not only did the canonists hold this, but also Pope Pius X, who in his Constitution *Promulgandi* said that those laws which were published solely in Rome were considered to have been promulgated everywhere in the world, and by such promulgation to have obtained the full force of law.[49]

[49] "Quae autem Romae, tamquam in christianae reipublicae centro et communi patria fidelium, promulgarentur, ea ubique gentium promulgata censebantur, vimque legis plenissimam obtinebant."—*AAS*, I (1909), 5.

Some authors held a sort of middle opinion in this matter, claiming that, when the popes in their constitutions explicitly stated that promulgation in Rome alone was sufficient for the universal binding power of the law, then that method of promulgation was sufficient. But in all other cases it was necessary that the law be promulgated in each diocese.[50]

This opinion is not acceptable, however, for the same reasons given in opposition to the rejected opinion that a promulgation in each diocese was necessary for every universal law of the Holy See. It is evident that, if the popes made explicit mention in their constitutions that the promulgation of a law by the publication of the text of the law in Rome alone served as an adequate promulgation for making the law binding on the universal Church, they did so not precisely for the sake of noting their use of an exceptional method of promulgation. For it was not by way of exception that the formulae which called for promulgation in Rome alone were found in the papal constitutions at the time when Sylvius (1581-1649) advanced his theory. The great majority of the papal constitutions which contained universal legislation ended with one of the formulae prescribing promulgation in Rome alone. And even if the laws did not contain such formulae, they were published in Rome alone just as the ones which did contain formulae that prescribed such an exclusively localized promulgation. This is clear from the record of promulgation appended to many of the constitutions.

Bouix by seeking to prove that promulgation was not of the essence of law, rather ambitiously tried to undermine the theory which upheld the necessity of diocesan promulgation, for he evidently felt that by so doing he could destroy the very foundation of this false theory.[51] It is, of course, true that the proponents of that theory did hold that promulgation was an essential element of law, but that view was held by a majority of the canonists from the fourteenth to the nineteenth century. In reality the question did not touch the essence of law; rather, it dealt with the nature of the promulgation of law. Did the act of promulgation when executed solely in Rome satisfy the notion

[50] Sylvius, *Commentarium in Summam Theologicam S. Thomae Aquinatis*, Q. 96, a. 4, quaer, xi, concl. 3.

[51] *De Principiis*, p. 233.

of the promulgation of law? On the one side some authors denied it; on the other side most authors affirmed it. So there was no quarrel among them over the theory of law or the need of a promulgation; rather, the contention centered on a point of fact, namely, whether the exclusive promulgation of law in Rome sufficed for the promulgation of a universally binding law.

Van Espen's argument in appeal to the earlier practice of the Church was inconclusive. In the chapter which treats of the history of the promulgation of pontifical legislation in the early centuries it was shown that the bishops of Rome did not always promulgate their laws by sending them to each diocese. Often they promulgated their laws in synods, and then sent notice of the promulgated laws to the bishops of the world. Centainly there is no proof that the early popes considered themselves bound to follow the civil law in this matter. As was shown before, there are texts which prove that they did consider their laws binding even in dioceses where they had not been promulgated. Furthermore, even if it had been the law of the ancient Church that universal legislation was to be promulgated in each diocese, the later popes could have changed the method of promulgation at will.

It may here prove suitable to advance a final objection to the theory of those who insisted that a diocesan promulgation was essential for the binding force of an enacted universal law. That objection derives from the fact of practical experience. Hostile rulers and obstinate bishops could have blocked papal legislation by forbidding or preventing the promulgation of it in their territory. That possibility was not merely a theoretical one. French kings did hinder the publishing of papal laws in France. Besides, the espoused theory led to a more serious error, namely, that the acceptance of ecclesiastical legislation was subject to the *placitum regis*.

Berutti adverts to another practical difficulty. Whenever a completely new diocese or prefecture or vicariate apostolic was constituted, a new act of promulgation of all the universal legislation of the Church would have been called for.[52] It is to be noted that such an act of promulgation would, of course,

[52] *Institutiones Iuris Canonici*, I, 66.

not have been demanded with every new creation of dioceses, vicariates and prefectures, for these were frequently created from portions of extant dioceses, vicariates and prefectures. Hence in such an event the laws which were already promulgated in the former diocese needed no longer to be promulgated in the territory of the newly constituted diocese. But the difficulty would have been relevant in the case of the discovery of a new land never known before, as in the case of the discovery of this country. Then, according to the viewpoint of the minority opinion, the laws would have had to be promulgated in this country before they became binding here, even if the discovery came decades after the institution of the laws.

CHAPTER V

The Constitution *Promulgandi*

On September 29, 1908, Pope Pius X issued the Constitution *Promulgandi,* which established as the official publication of the Holy See the *Commentarium Officiale de Apostolicae Sedis Actis.*[1] By this act the pope established for the first time in the history of the Church an exclusive and prescribed method for promulgating the laws of the Holy See. Previous to 1908 there had been several publications in which new legislation was reported. The *Acta Sanctae Sedis* had been published since 1865, but official recognition was given only on May 23, 1904, when Pius X declared it authentic and approved it officially as a means for the publishing of the acts of the Holy See.[2]

Volume XXXVII (1904-1905) was the first volume to enjoy a fully authentic character. But even so the approval accorded by the Holy See did not make the act of publication in the periodical an act of promulgation. All that the official approval meant was that in the future such acts and decrees as would be printed in this periodical were to be considered as authentic. So the *Acta Sanctae Sedis* became a means for publicizing those constitutions and laws which had been already promulgated in the usual way. This is deducible from the words of the letter of approval. In this letter the *Acta Sanctae Sedis* was declared an authentic and official periodical for making public the acts of the Apostolic See. The letter did not state that the periodical was the means for the promulgation of the laws of the Holy See. Furthermore, it is in this way that the editors of the maga-

1 *AAS,* I (1909), 5.

2 Ex Audientia SSmi habita die 23 Maii 1904.

Sanctissimus Dominus Noster Pius divina providentia Papa X, referente me infrascripto Sacrae Congregationis de Propaganda Fide Cardinali Praefecto, precibus benigne annuens, memoratas ephemerides authenticas et officiales Apostolicae Sedis Actis publice evulgandis declaravit. . . .

F.H.M. Card. GOTTI, Praefectus.

—*Acta Sanctae Sedis* (41 vols., Romae, 1865-1908), XXXVII (1904-1905), 5 (hereafter cited *ASS*).

zine understood the papal approval, for in their public message of thanks to the Holy Father they asserted that the *Acta Sanctae Sedis* would effect not the promulgation of the acts of the Apostolic See but rather the divulgation of these acts.[3] A final evidence of this is found in the fact that in the Constitution *Promulgandi* Pope Pius X did not refer to the *Acta Sanctae Sedis* when he spoke of the means of promulgation used previously in the Church.

Some authors state that from the year 1870 the Holy See was accustomed to promulgate laws by means of a publication of the law in the periodical *Acta Sanctae Sedis.*[4] Coronata says that *de facto* this was the means of promulgation that was used after the year 1870. He adds that Maroto states that after May 23, 1904, such publication in the *Acta Sanctae Sedis* was *de iure* the method used for promulgating the laws of the Holy See.[5] However, Maroto does not seem to say this. He merely explains the method of promulgation through the publication of the law in the office of the Secretary of a Roman congregation.

It is clear that before 1909 there was no law determining an exclusive method of promulgating pontifical legislation. Pope Pius X did not make the *Acta Sanctae Sedis* a means of promulgating pontifical law, and this is evident from the fact that, although the Constitution *Promulgandi* was issued only four years and four months after the papal approval was given to the *Acta Sanctae Sedis* by the same pope, no mention was made in this constitution that the *Acta Sanctae Sedis* had been a means of promulgating ecclesiastical legislation. Furthermore, if the *Acta Sanctae Sedis* had been the means of the official promulgation of the laws of the Holy See, no new enactment would have been necessary. The Constitution *Promulgandi* would not have been needed.

In the Constitution *Promulgandi* the pope explained that through the centuries the manner of promulgating pontifical constitutions and laws had not always been the same. He then

[3] ". . . cum nobis compertum sit eo magis hac Pontificia declaratione Ephemerides in bonum totius christianae societatis . . . redundare, quo maior necessitas urget Acta Apostolicae Sedis per universum orbem Apostolica quoque Auctoritate divulgentur . . ." —ASS, XXXVII (1904-1905), 4.

[4] Coronata, *Institutiones Iuris Canonici,* I, 20; Cicognani, *Canon Law,* p. 552.

[5] Coronata, *Institutiones Iuris Canonici,* I, 20, ftn. 1.

spoke briefly of the methods of promulgation formerly used in the Church, affirming that when laws had been published in the public places in Rome, they were considered to be promulgated everywhere in the world and thus obtained the full force of law. But since the manner of promulgation depended on the will of the legislator, this method of promulgation was not the only one ever used in the Church. The Pontiff mentioned one other method which more recently had become a customary usage in Rome. The acts of the Roman Congregations, to whom the popes had given power to interpret the extant law and even to make new laws, were considered promulgated when by legitimate authority they were published in the office of the Secretary by whom they were issued, especially since this manner of promulgation enjoyed the express or tacit approval of the Holy Father.

However, many bishops had petitioned not only Pius X but also his predecessors that some publication be established in which the new laws of the Holy See would be promulgated and the acts of the Apostolic See published. This was accomplished by Pius X when he established as the official publication of the Holy See the *Acta Apostolicae Sedis*. Laws, decrees and pontifical constitutions were to be promulgated by being published in this periodical, and this was to constitute the exclusive method of their publication unless the Holy See provided otherwise. No provision was made regarding any length of time during which the subjects were not bound by the newly promulgated law. Furthermore, in order that the promulgation be legitimate, it was necessary that the publication of a law in the *Acta* had been ordered by a competent prelate, usually the Secretary of the Congregation issuing the law. Of course, this condition was presumed to have been fulfilled if the document appeared in the *Acta*.

A few years after the establishment of the *Acta Apostolicae Sedis* as the one means of promulgation there was a case in which the Holy See did provide for promulgation in a different manner. A collection was made of all the acts of Pius X which contained the laws and decrees issued by him before 1909, since these had not been promulgated in the official publication. This collection, known as *Pii X Pontificis Maximi Acta,*[6] was officially approved; all that was contained therein was declared authentic on December 26, 1913, in a letter issued by the Cardinal Secretary of State, Raphael Cardinal Merry del Val.[7]

The text of the letter mentions four volumes, but the fifth volume is really included, since it is nothing more than the second part of Volume IV. Furthermore, the letter stated: "Completa nuper editione voluminum quae *Acta Pii X* inscribuntur. . . ."[8]

Since the pope declared that by the act of their publication in this collection the laws and constitutions were to be considered promulgated just as if they had been published in the *Acta,* he evidently invoked an exceptional method of promulgation, which he used in this particular instance only. This exceptional method recalls to mind the method used by the popes of the thirteenth and fourteenth centuries, when they gathered decretal letters into a collection and then promulgated the collection by sending it to the universities. However, the collection of the acts of Pius X was not promulgated as a collection; rather, by the very fact that his laws and constitutions were published in this collection they were officially promulgated. Thus the collection itself was a means for the promulgation of the papal legisation.

The method of promulgation prescribed by the Constitution *Promulgandi* was used for the promulgation of the new Code of Canon Law. The Code was promulgated with the papal bull of promulgation, the Constitution *Providentissima Mater Ecclesia*

---

[6] 5 vols., Romae, 1905-1913.

[7] Secretaria Status
De Promulgatione Quarumdam Pontificiarum
Constitutionum ac Legum.
Ex audientia Sanctissimi, die 26 decembris 1913.

Completa nuper editione voluminum quae *Acta Pii X* inscribuntur, ad dubitationem quamlibet praecavendam de legitima promulgatione Pontificiarum constitutionum ac legum in iis insertarum, Ssmus Dñus noster Pius divina Providentia PP. X, referente me infrascripto Cardinali a Secretis Status, decernere dignatus est: omnes ac singulas Constitutiones ac leges, in quatuor praedictorum *Actorum* voluminibus contentas, plenissime promulgatas atque idcirco ratas firmasque habendas esse, perinde ac si in commentario officiali "*Acta Apostolicae Sedis*" insertae verbo ad verbum fuissent. Contrariis quibusvis etiam speciali ac individua mentione dignis minime obstantibus.

Datum Romae, e Secretaria Status, die, mense et anno praedictis.

R. Card. Merry del Val.

—*AAS*, V (1913), 558.

[8] Lijdsman, *Introductio in Jus Canonicum,* p. 383.

of Pope Benedict XV, May 27, 1917, by being published in the *Acta Apostolicae Sedis.*[9] An appendix containing the corrections of errors which appeared in the original edition of the Code together with the Motu Proprio *Cum Iuris Canonici* and an analytico-alphabetical index, was promulgated in the *Acta* in a supplement to Volume IX, Part II, issued on December 31, 1917. The bull of promulgation provided for a period of a full liturgical year—Pentecost, 1917 to Pentecost, 1918—before the Code became binding on May 19, 1918.

In order to enable readers readily to distinguish between those documents which are to be considered as laws and those that are not published as laws, the Secretariate of State on January 5, 1910, ordered that this periodical be divided thenceforth into two sections, the one an official section reserved for laws, the other an illustrative section adapted for jurisprudence.[10] It is to be observed that up to the present time that division has not yet been introduced. Van Hove gives the following norm for deciding whether or not texts in the *Acta* are to be considered as laws. As long as the requisites for a law are present, namely, those requisites that pertain to the matter and the legislative power of the author, and if the document is inscribed "*Dubia*" or "*Decretum,*" it is to be considered a law. Not to be considered as laws are those documents which are inscribed "*Romana et aliorum,*" or "*Dioecesis N.,*" etc.[11]

[9] Vol. IX (1917), pars II.
[10] AAS, II (1910), 37.
[11] *De Legibus,* p. 138.

CHAPTER VI

The Promulgation of Universal Pontifical Legislation According to the Code of Canon Law

The law of the Constitution *Promulgandi* was adopted into the Code of Canon Law without any changes being prescribed regarding the method to be used in the promulgation of laws of the Holy See. Canon 9 states: "Leges ab Apostolica Sede latae promulgantur per editionem in *Actorum Apostolicae Sedis commentario officiali*, nisi in casibus particularibus alius promulgandi modus fuerit praescriptus; . . ."

This canon refers to all laws that emanate from the Holy See, whether they be universal or particular. The term Apostolic See, as used in the quoted canon, is to be interpreted according to canon 7; and includes besides the Holy Father himself, the Congregations, Tribunals and Offices of the Roman Curia in the event that a law should be issued through one of these. Furthermore, since the canon uses the word *leges*, only laws are subject to the methods of promulgation prescribed; decrees, rescripts, etc., are not included, unless they contain true laws.

A term in canon 9 that is open to possible misunderstanding is the term *editio*.[1] It is not sufficient for the publication of a law in the *Acta* that the text of the law be printed in the *Acta*. The term publication (*editio*) as used in this canon means more than a mere printing. The notion of publication includes besides the printing of the law also a public distribution of the copies of the *Acta*; there must be some presentation to the public.[2]

Since the law of canon 9 is a restatement of the pre-Code law, this law must be interpreted according to the words of the Constitution *Promulgandi*.[3] This constitution required two things, that the law be inserted in the *Acta Apostolicae Sedis* and that

[1] In this chapter the Latin *editio* is rendered with the English "publication."

[2] Cf. Van Hove, *De Legibus*, p. 137; Maroto, *Institutiones Iuris Canonici*, I, 197; Berutti, *Institutiones Iuris Canonici*, I, 63.

[3] Canon 6, 2°.

it be put before the public, clearly showing that the mere printing was not enough.[4]

From what has been said concerning the nature of promulgation as also from the words of the Constitution *Promulgandi* and of canon 9 of the Code of Canon Law, it is clear that at the present time a law is considered promulgated when the number of the *Acta* in which the law appears has been released to the public. It is not necessary that all the copies of that particular issue of the *Acta* be distributed. As long as the particular number of the *Acta* which contains the law has been released to the public in such a way that from this public release it is morally possible for all those affected by the law to receive notice of the law, the publication can be said to have taken place. It is possible that the promulgation of a law could be accomplished if only one copy of the *Acta* were printed and made public, as long as that were done in such a way that all the Catholic world could know of the law from this publication.

Maroto adds that the promulgation of the law is presumed to take place on the date that is printed on the cover of the copy of the *Acta* in which the text of the law appears.[5] It is presumed that the copies of the *Acta* were distributed on that day.

The Code recognizes that in a particular case another method of promulgation might be more effective. Consequently, the Holy See has reserved to itself the right to prescribe an exceptional method of promulgation in a particular instance. It is clear, however, from the text of canon 9 that no exceptional method is to be presumed, nor is one to be used unless it be expressly prescribed. If no mention is made by the Holy See of the method of promulgation to be used in the case of a new law, then the ordinary method of promulgation by means of publication in the *Acta Apostolicae Sedis* is to be employed.

Michiels declares that the Sacred Congregation of the Sacraments required that its decree containing laws concerning the

[4] "Volumus autem Constitutiones pontificias, leges, decreta, aliaque tum Romanorum Pontificum tum sacrarum Congregationum et Officiorum scita, in eo Commentario de mandato Praelati a secretis aut maioris administri eius Congregationis vel Officii, a quo illa dimanent, inserta et in vulgus edita, hac una, eaque unica ratione legitime promulgata haberi. . . ."—*AAS*, I (1909), 6.

[5] *Institutiones Iuris Canonici*, I, 197.

frequent renewal of the sacred hosts (December 7, 1918)[6] be published in all diocesan newspapers. He calls this, however, not a special promulgation of this decree, but a greater divulgation of the decree.[7] It is clear that no special method of promulgation was prescribed by the Sacred Congregation in the decree itself. Nor is their any evidence in the *Acta*[8] that any special method of promulgation was ordered. Therefore, the publication of this decree in the diocesan newspapers was to be considered not as a method of promulgation, but rather as a method used for bringing the decree to the notice of the entire clergy. There seems to be no example of an exceptional method of promulgation invoked since the law of the Code has been in force.

The Code provides for a penalty of automatic excommunication, reserved for its absolution in a special way to the Holy Father, and incurred by one who directly or indirectly prohibits the promulgation of a law of the Holy See.[9] This penalty is not one that is enacted for the first time through the law of the Code. The present legislation is a restatement of the law of the Constitution *Apostolicae Sedis* of Pope Pius IX.[10]

As to the meaning of the word *prohibentes* the authors do not uniformly agree. A number say that this term includes all who hinder or prohibit the promulgation of the acts of the Holy See, including private persons, since the law makes no distinction.[11] Coronata claims that this is the more common opinion, but actually more authors hold the opposite, namely, that only those who by virtue of a public power, e.g., governors or kings or postal authorities make such a prohibition against the promulgation of the laws of the Holy See incur this penalty.[12] This prohibition must be effected by means of some positive act.

[6] *AAS*, XI (1919), 8.

[7] *Normae Generales Juris Canonici*, I, 238.

[8] *AAS*, IX (1919), 8.

[9] Canon 2333: "Recurrentes ad laicam potestatem ad impediendas litteras vel acta quaelibet a Sede Apostolica vel ab eiusdem Legatis profecta, eorumve promulgationem vel exsecutionem directe vel indirecte prohibentes, . . . ipso facto subiaceant excommunicationi Sedi Apostolicae speciali modo reservatae."

[10] §1, n. 8—*Fontes*, n. 552.

[11] Cf. Coronata, *Institutiones Iuris Canonici*, IV, 376.

[12] Cf. Chelodi, *Ius Canonicum de Delictis et Poenis et de Iudiciis Criminalibus* (5.ed. recognita et aucta a Pio Ciprotti, Vicenza: Societá Anonima Tipografica, 1943), p. 92 (hereafter cited as *De Delictis et Poenis*); Ayrinhac, *Penal Legislation in the New Code of Canon Law*, (Revised by Rev. P. J. Lydon, New York: Benziger Bros., 1944), p. 194; Beste, *Introductio in Codicem*, p. 944; Vermeersch-Creusen, *Epitome Iuris Canonici*, III, n. 533; Sole, *De Delictis et Poenis* (Romae: Pustet, 1920), p. 262.

A direct prohibition would be one that is effected by means of a law or a decree forbidding the promulgation of the laws of the Holy See, or by means of an act of the civil authority which in any way prevents those things from being done which are necessary for the promulgating of the law. Guilty of an indirect prohibition would be those who, although they do not themselves enjoy public power, induce the civil authorities to prohibit the promulgation of the laws of the Holy See.[13]

That the term promulgation as incorporated in canon 2333 does not at the same time comprise the notion of the divulgation of the law seems deducible for two reasons. First, canon 2228 insists that a penalty enacted in law is not incurred unless according to the proper signification inherent in the wording of the law the specifically categorized delict was fully and completely perpetrated. To associate the incurring of the penalty with those who hinder the divulgation, and not simply the promulgation, would be to depart from the norm which demands advertence to the proper meaning of the term promulgation. Secondly, canon 2219, §1, establishes the firm principle that in penal law a benign rather than a harsh interpretation is to obtain.

But, granted that the concepts of promulgation and divulgation are not to be identified in canon 2333, such as hinder the divulgation of a law are nevertheless subject to the enacted penalty inasmuch as their acts of hindrance involve at the same time at least an indirect prevention of the execution of the papal document, or imply an act of recourse to the lay power for the purpose of impeding it, or entail either harm or threat for those to whom the document is directed, or also to others. The point at issue is not that no penalty is incurred by those who hinder the divulgation of a law already promulgated, but that, if the penalty be incurred, it is not in consequence of the law which enacts a penalty for those who prevent the promulgation of the law.

Some authors are ready to assume for the term promulgation as employed in canon 2333 a wider meaning than its technical one, namely, when there is question of papal letters, acts or

[13] Wernz-Vidal, *Ius Canonicum*, VII, 479; Chelodi, *De Delicitis et Poenis*, p. 92; Coronata, *Institutiones Iuris Canonici*, IV, p. 376.

documents which do not call for a promulgation in the strict sense.[14] It is only when these are of the nature of legislation than an act of promulgation is called for. Accordingly, so these authors contend, the term promulgation in relation to such letters, acts and documents should be understood as pointing also to their divulgation, publication and intimation. But, since the direct and also the indirect prevention of the execution of these documents, and other similar acts of hindrance, harm, or threat likewise stand penalized in canon 2333, there seems to be better juridical reason that one or the other of these categories will cover the case of those who prevent the divulgation of a papal documents or act, than that these same delinquents should be classified under those who prevent the act of promulgation. The term promulgation is given a closely fixed meaning in the Code. It seems untenable, especially in penal law, to assign to this term or to assume for it a meaning that lies outside of this fixed limit.

In the event that the civil authority did prohibit the promulgation of the laws of the Holy See, but the law was promulgated in spite of this prohibition, it is not agreed that the censure is then incurred. It seems that the censure would be incurred if there was enacted a law which prohited the promulgation of the laws of the Holy See, for there would be a real prohibition, even though the civil law were evaded and the promulgation of the ecclesiastical law were accomplished. However, if the word *prohibens* is to be taken in the sense of an actual prevention of the promulgation of the papal law, then the censure would not be incurred unless the promulgation of the law had actually been prevented. Considering the word *prohibere* as it is usually used, one would say that the prohibition is realized as soon as a decree has been issued or a mandate given in order to forbid or to hinder the promulgation of the laws of the Holy See, even though it may never happen that the promulgation of the laws is actually prevented. Cappello declares that the solution of this problem will come only when the true meaning of the term *prohibens* has been established.[15]

---

[14] Cf., e.g., Coronata, *Institutiones Iuris Canonici,* IV, 377, who lists other authors sharing his own view.

[15] *Tractatus Canonico-Moralis De Censuris* (3.ed., Taurinorum Augustae: Marietti, 1933), p. 233.

CHAPTER VII

The Promulgation of Conciliar Legislation

ARTICLE 1

Laws of the Ecumenical Councils

Laws directly enacted by the Roman Pontiffs are not the only universal legislation in the Church; there is also another source of universal law, the general council. While it is true that these councils have no authority over the universal Church unless they have been approved and confirmed by the Roman Pontiff, still, when their decrees have received this papal confirmation, they are constituted as laws and as such must be promulgated to become binding. It is accordingly a matter of historical interest to examine the manner in which such laws were promulgated throughout the centuries.

All the early general councils, the first eight to be exact, were held in the East. Over none of these did the pope preside personally. Hence the papal approval or confirmation of the decrees always came subsequently to the celebration of the councils. The method to be employed in making the decrees known was indicated in a number of cases, but it is not certain that the use of this method constituted an official promulgation of the decrees. Rather, authors generally hold that the disciplinary decrees of the first eight general councils were promulgated in the conciliar sessions.[1]

The decrees of the VI Ecumenical Council, that is, the III General Council of Constantinople (680-681), were sent by Pope Leo II (682-683) to the bishops of Spain with the instruction that the acts should be made known to all the priests and people.[2] It is true that the notion of promulgation was not at all

[1] E.g., Van Hove, *De Legibus*, p. 135; Lijdsman (*Introductio in Jus Canonicum*, p. 414), although not explicit, seems to say the same thing.

[2] "Ut per universos vestrae provinciae Praesules, sacerdotes et plebes, per religiosum vestrum studium innotescat, ac salubriter divulgetur."—Mansi, XI, 1052.

clear at that time. In consequence terms were not used with the same technical meaning that attaches to them at present. But since the text in question refers to the publication of a law that had already been promulgated, the use of the word *divulgetur* represented a very exact usage; it was the term that would be used today for conveying the same particular idea.

Beginning with the General Councils of the Lateran a new factor was evident. For the first time the pope personally presided over the general council, and his confirmation was given to the laws as they were enacted in the sessions of the council. In the case of these councils the decrees were certainly promulgated in the solemn conciliar sessions. Wernz (1842-1914) taught that the promulgation of the laws coincided with the papal confirmation in these cases.[3] This truly obtained at the time, but the two notions should nevertheless not be identified, for certainly the confirmation and the promulgation were not the same, although they could be effected by one and the same act, as was evidently done in repeated instances.

The I General Council of the Lateran (1123) was presided over by Pope Calixtus II (1119-1124), and it was by him that the laws of the Council were confirmed in the solemn sessions.[4] The decrees of the II General Council of the Lateran, presided over by Pope Innocent II (1130-1143) in 1139, were promulgated in the same way, and in like manner also those of the III General Council of the Lateran (1179) under Alexander III (1159-1181),[5] and of the IV General Council of the Lateran (1215) under Pope Innocent III (1198-1216). An exceptional form of promulgation was prescribed for one of the canons of this Council, namely, can. xxii, *Cum infirmitas*,[6] which enacted a penalty for doctors who failed to call a priest for a dying patient.[7] Since the pope declared that the law did not bind until it had been published by the local prelates, this law needed a diocesan promulgation before it took effect.

[3] *Ius Decretalium*, I, n. 180.

[4] Mansi, XXI, 297.

[5] "His itaque decretis promulgatis, et ab universo clero ac populo circumstante receptis."—Mansi, XXII, 234.

[6] C. 13, X, *de poenitentiis et remissionibus*, V, 38.

[7] "Si quis autem medicorum huius nostrae constitutionis, postquam per praelatos locorum fuerit publicata, transgressor extiterit, tam diu ab ingressu ecclesiae arceatur donec pro transgressione huiusmodi satisfacerit competenter."—Mansi, XXII, 1010.

Pope Innocent IV (1243-1254) sent the legislation of the I General Council of Lyons (1245) with the Bull "*Cum nuper*"[8] to the University of Bologna, thus promulgating that compilation of laws. The legislation of the II General Council of Lyons (1274) was also promulgated by being sent to the university as a collection. Whether or not the laws of these two councils were previously promulgated in the conciliar sessions is not certain, but it is possible that they were, so that the subsequent official transmission of the conciliar legislation to the universities was but the promulgation of the new compilations.

The Council of Vienne (1311-1312) issued a number of disciplinary decrees which Pope Clement V (1305-1314) intended to incorporate in a compilation together with other of his decrees and constitutions. He died before he could achieve his purpose, but the work was finished by his successor, John XXII (1316-1334), and the compilation was sent to the universities in the same manner as the decrees of the previous two general councils had been sent.

The Councils of Constance (1414-1418) and of Basle-Ferrara-Florence (1431-1449) were only partly ecumenical in character. The decrees were not confirmed in the solemn sessions except when the pope presided. Subsequent confirmation and promulgation were necessary in relation to such sessions over which the pope did not preside. The decrees of the V General Council of the Lateran (1512-1517), over the sessions of which at first Pope Julius II (1503-1513) and later Pope Leo X (1513-1521) presided, were read to the assembled fathers, and later posted in the usual places in the city of Rome, on the doors of the Basilicas of Saint Peter and of Saint John Lateran, on the doors of the Apostolic Chancery, and likewise in the Campo di Fiori.[9]

The Council of Trent (1545-1563) was not presided over by any of the popes in person. Accordingly the decrees of the Council were presented to Pope Pius IV (1559-1565) for confirmation in secret consistory. On January 26, 1564, this pope issued the Bull "*Benedictus Deus,*" in which he announced the confirmation of the acts of the Council of Trent, and ordered

[8] Mansi, XXIII, 651.
[9] Mansi, XXXII, 716.

them to be promulgated by being first read in the churches of Saint Peter and of Saint John Lateran, and then by being posted on the doors of these Basilicas, on the portals of the Apostolic Chancery, and in the Campo di Fiori.[10]

For one of the decrees of this Council a special form of promulgation was prescribed. The Decree *Tametsi* had to be promulgated in every parish, and it did not bind in a parish until thirty days after the first publication in that parish.[11]

The last of the ecumenical councils, the Vatican Council (1869-1870), issued no disciplinary decrees. The dogmatic definitions of the Council were solemnly promulgated in the conciliar sessions by Pope Pius IX (1846-1876), and later were posted in the usual places in the city of Rome.

The law of the Code does not determine the method to be used in the promulgating of the decrees of future ecumenical councils. However, the Code does declare that the decrees of a general council are to be promulgated at the command of the Roman Pontiff.[12]

Article 2

The Legislation of Plenary and Provincial Councils

The laws of other councils, not general in nature but either national or provincial, presented a slightly different problem as far as their promulgation was concerned. For such laws the members of the council could provide any method of promulgation which they considered best. Even now under the law of the Code no uniform way of promulgating particular conciliar law is prescribed.[13]

Relative to the early centuries of the Christian era, although many councils were held in various parts of the world and their

---

[10] *Bullarium*, VII, 244.

[11] Conc. Trident., sess. xxiv, *de ref. matrim.*, c. 1: "Ne vero haec tam salubria praecepta quemquam lateant, ordinariis omnibus praecipit, ut, quam primum potuerint, curent hoc decretum populo publicari ac explicari in singulis suarum dioecesum parochialibus ecclesiis, idque in primo anno quam saepissime fiat, deinde vero quoties expedire viderint.

"Decernit insuper, ut hujusmodi decretum in unaquaque parochia suum robur post triginta dies habere incipiat, a die primae publicationis, in eadem parochia factae, numerandos."

[12] Canon 227: "Concilii decreta vim definitivam obligandi non habent, nisi a Romano Pontifice fuerint confirmata et eius iussu promulgata.

[13] Canon 291, §1: ". . . ipsimet autem Concilii Patres designent et modum promulgationis decretorum et tempus quo decreta promulgata obligare incipiant."

laws were certainly promulgated, there is no way of knowing for certain what methods were habitually employed. It seems certain that frequently the laws were promulgated in the sessions of the councils themselves. For example, Archbishop Otto of Milan in September, 1287, promulgated a number of canons in a reform council.[14] It is known, however, that the laws were always published in such a way that all who were to be bound by them could learn of them. The fathers of the III Council of Carthage (397) gave evidence of their concern in this matter. They decreed in a letter that the canons were to be made known to everyone in the province.[15]

Herard, Archbishop of Tours, in 858 presided over a provincial council, and then ordered certain of the chapters to be read publicly to the priests of the parishes in order that all might know of them.[16] The council held at Vienna in the year 1267 ordered that its acts be read in the diocesan and provincial synods in that country, and commanded that the things which pertained to the laity should be published in each diocese in the parish churches.[17]

The promulgation or publication in each parish church of the new legislation of particular councils was in common usage for many centuries. The use of other means was also current. At times the new laws were announced to the public by town-criers, or again, in imitation of the method employed in the promulgation of papal legislation, the text of the new law was posted in a public place. Thus in 1355 the Archbishop of Prague, in statute 68 of a provincial council, ordered the various collegiate chapters to publish the laws by attaching a copy of them to a small chain in a public place in the capitular church, and to leave it there for three months.[18] Regarding the promulgation of particular law in the public places there was no controversy, as there was regarding the promulgation of papal legislation. All

[14] Hefele, *Histoire des Conciles*, nouvelle traduction par Dom. H. Leclercq (10 vols. in 19, Paris, 1907-1938), VI, premiere partie, 316.

[15] "Haec communi consilio per universam provinciam Byzacenam in notitiam cunctis deducenda censuimus."—Hardouin, *Acta Conciliorum et Epistolae Decretales ac Constitutiones Summorum Pontificum* (12 vols., Parisiis, 1714-1715), I, 969.

[16] Mansi, XV, 525.

[17] Mansi, XXIII, 1176.

[18] Mansi, XXVI, 383.

the canonists agreed that for the promulgation of the laws of ordinaries or of provincial councils a promulgation in the see or metropolitan city was sufficient for the valid promulgation of the law.[19]

In the nineteenth century several provincial councils decreed the exact methods that were to be used for the promulgation of the decrees of these councils. A provincial council of Ravenna (1855) ordered that its decrees, once they had been approved by the Holy See, were to be promulgated by being posted first on the doors of the metropolitan church, and then on the doors of all the cathedral and collegiate churches in the province.[20]

The III Provincial Council of Quebec (1863) ordered that its decrees be promulgated, after they had been approved by the Holy See, by each bishop either in a diocesan synod or else, if a synod could not be held, outside a synod as soon as possible.[21]

In this country the fathers of the III Plenary Council of Baltimore (1884) in the sessions of the Council agreed on the method that was to be used, once the approval of the Holy See had been obtained, for promulgating the laws of this Plenary Council. The laws of the Council were to be promulgated by the Apostolic Delegate, James Cardinal Gibbons, and they were to become binding as soon as he had promulgated them. As a precautionary measure, however, and as an aid to insuring their divulgation, the fathers of the Council urged that, as soon as possible after the promulgation by the Cardinal, the promulgation of the conciliar legislation should be reiterated in provincial and diocesan synods.[22] The decree of promulgation followed a little more than a year later, on January 6, 1886.

---

19 Bouix, *De Principiis*, p. 236.

20 Cap. X, §2: ". . . edicimus, ut, postquam haec ab Apostolica Sede probata fuerint, edantur et in valvis proponantur primum ecclesiae metropolitanae, deinde omnium cathedralium et collegiatarum provinciae; . . .—*Acta et Decreta Sacrorum Conciliorum Recentiorum, Collectio Lacensis* (7 vols., *Friburgi Brisgoviae*, 1870-1890), VI, 211, d. (hereafter cited as *Coll. Lac.*).

21 C. 13: "Decreta hujus Synodi provincialis nemo prelo subjiciat aut promulget, antequam a Sancta Sede Apostolica, . . . revisa et recognita fuerint. Litteris autem quibus illa confirmentur a Sanctitate Sua obtentis, ea statim imprimantur, impressaque, a singulis Episcopis, vel in Synodo dioecesana, vel, si celebrari nequeat, extra Synodum, quam primum promulgentur."—*Coll. Lac.*, III, 679, a.

22 *Acta et Decreta Concilii Plenarii Baltimorensis Tertii* (Baltimorae: Murphy, 1886), p. 184.

The Code of Canon Law demands that all acts and decrees of plenary and provincial councils are to be sent by the presiding prelate at the conclusion of the council to the Holy See. These acts and decrees may not be promulgated before they have been reviewed by the Holy See, but it is the fathers of the council who determine what method is to be used in promulgating their decrees.[23] From the words of canon 291, §1, it can be seen that the Code expects the method of the promulgation of the decrees of the plenary or provincial council to be designated by the fathers assembled in council. However, there is nothing in the Code that prevents this designation from being made later on, as long as the method is chosen by the fathers of the council. It would be possible, therefore, that, after the papal approbation has been received, the fathers should reassemble and then designate a method of promulgation.

No special method for promulgating the decrees of a plenary or provincial council is even suggested in the Code. Any adequate method of promulgation, then, can be chosen by the fathers of the council. Usually such decrees are promulgated either in diocesan synods held after the approval of the Holy See has been received, or through the publication of the decrees in book form, through a public announcement in the churches, or through the act of publication in the diocesan papers.[24] The law of the Code concerning the method of promulgation of the decrees of plenary and provincial councils[25] refers also to those plenary or regional or provincial councils which are held in regions subject to the Sacred Congregation for the Propagation of the Faith.[26]

In the year 1920, a provincial council was held in the city of Mechlin (Malines) and presided over by Cardinal Mercier. The assembled fathers concluded the acts of the Council with a statement of the method which was to be used in promulgating the

[23] Canon 291, §1: "Absoluto Concilio plenario aut provinciali, praeses acta et decreta omnia ad Sanctam Sedem transmittat, nec eadem antea promulgentur, quam a Sacra Congregatione Concilii expensa et recognita fuerint; ipsimet autem Concilii Patres designent et modum promulgationis decretorum et tempus quo decreta promulgata obligare incipiant."

[24] Cf. Cappello, *Summa Iuris Canonici,* I, 79.

[25] Canon 291, §1.

[26] Canon 304, §2.

decrees after the papal recognition had been received. It was decided that each bishop was to promulgate the decrees in his own diocese in the same way in which he ordinarily promulgated his own episcopal legislation.[27] After the decree of recognition had been received from Rome (November 16, 1922), a decree of promulgation was issued by the fathers of the Provincial Council on March 25, 1923.

The fathers of the IV Provincial Council of Portland, Oregon (1932), issued a decree of promulgation on July 20, 1934, almost two years after the Council was held, and just six months after the papal permission was given. The decree of promulgation stated merely that they promulgated the decrees of the Council and made no mention of the method used in promulgating the decrees.[28] Evidently the fathers of the Council had agreed on some method for the promulgation of their decrees. Probably it was through the publication of the volume containing these decrees.

A provincial council was held in Toronto in 1938. At the conclusion of the Council, but while yet assembled, the fathers issued the decree of promulgation (December 15, 1938), and in that decree the method of the promulgation of the decrees is stated. The decrees were to be published in an official edition by the metropolitan, the ordinary of the archdiocese of Toronto.[29]

---

[27] *Acta et Decreta Concilii Provincialis Mechliniensis Quarti anno MCMXX Mechliniae Habiti* (Mechliniae: H. Dessain, 1923), p. 156.

[28] ". . . Decreta Concilii provincialis Portlandensis, in Oregon Quarti, ab Apostolica Sede recognita, auctoritate nostra promulgamus . . ."—*Acta et Decreta Concilii Provincialis Portlandensis in Oregon Quarti, anno 1932* (Portland, Oregon: Sentinel Printery, 1934), p. 11.

[29] *Acta et Decreta Concilii Provincialis Torontini Secundi* (Toronto, 1938), p. 83.

CHAPTER VIII

The Promulgation of Episcopal Law

The Code in two distinct canons mentions the methods for the promulgation of law enacted by episcopal ordinaries. First, the laws made by bishops alone outside a diocesan synod are mentioned in canon 335, §2: "Leges episcopales statim a promulgatione obligare incipiunt, nisi aliud in ipsis caveatur; modus autem promulgationis ab ipsomet episcopo determinatur."

In the case, then, of episcopal legislation enacted outside a diocesan synod, the bishop is entirely free to choose any adequate method of promulgating his law. Previously it was mentioned that the method of promulgation is not determined by the nature of law, and therefore it is the lawmaker's right to designate any method of promulgation by which he presents the law to the community of his subjects in such a way that it is humanly possible for all to receive notice of the law.

There are various methods which have been used for effecting the promulgation of such episcopal law. As has been seen before, in the early history of the Church episcopal laws were promulgated either in a diocesan synod, especially if they pertained solely to the clergy, or by a public reading either in the cathedral church only or in all the churches of the diocese. Some bishops, too, imitated the method of promulgation used by the popes between the fourteenth and twentieth centuries. They promulgated their laws by attaching a copy of the law to the doors of the cathedral church or to the doors of other churches.

At present, in the post-Code era, several methods are used for the promulgation of extra-synodal episcopal law. One method for the promulgation of this type of legislation is the publication of the new law in the diocesan newspaper. Another method used quite frequently is the sending of a letter by the bishop to all the pastors or even to all the priests in the diocese. For example, on December 1, 1945, the archbishop of Cincinnati sent a letter to all the priests of his archdiocese, promulgating a decree which forbade any priest to speak over the radio within the limits of the archdiocese on matters pertaining to faith or morals if he had not previously submitted his manuscript to the chancery. This decree was also published in the diocesan newspaper.[1] Sometimes laws affecting all the faithful are promulgated by being read in all the churches. A valid method of promulgation would be an announcement of the law over the radio, although the writer knows of no case in which this has been done. Also, the old method of promulgation by means of a public posting of the text of the law could be used for the purpose of promulgating episcopal legislation.

Secondly, the Code considers laws made by bishops in diocesan synods. Canon 362 states: "Unicus est in Synodo legislator Episcopus, ceteris votum tantum consultivum habentibus; unus ipse subscribit synodalibus constitutionibus; quae, si in Synodo promulgentur, eo ipso obligare incipiunt, nisi aliud expresse caveatur." It can be noted that, even though canon 362 indicates a method of promulgation for the synodal legislation, this method is not obligatory. The bishop is free to choose any method for the promulgation of the synodal decrees, but if he chooses the one method mentioned here—promulgation in the synod itself—then the laws are presumed to bind immediately unless the contrary is expressly stated.

In the case of the diocesan synod no approval of the Holy See for the decrees of the synod is required. Hence, the bishop does not have to wait for a time before he can promulgate his decrees, as the fathers of a plenary or provincial council must wait. Therefore, the method of promulgation within the synod is feasible and quite convenient for the ordinary. The laws of the V Synod of the Diocese of Brooklyn (February 25, 26, 1926) were promulgated in the sessions of the synod itself,[2] as also were the decrees of the IX Synod of Harrisburg (December 16, 1943).[3] This same method of promulgation was also used for

[1] The Catholic Telegraph-Register (Cincinnati, 1831-), Vol. CXIV, n. 8 (Dec. 7, 1945), p. 1.

[2] *Constitutiones Dioecesanae Brooklynienses* (New York: Loughlin Bros., 1926), p. i.

[3] *Ninth Synod of the Diocese of Harrisburg* (Harrisburg, 1944), p. xxiv.

the promulgation of the decrees of the I Synod of the Diocese of Fargo (September 29, 30, 1941). In his decree of promulgation, issued on the last day of the synod, the bishop declared that the laws of the synod were binding immediately from that day onward. By this statement he showed that the decrees had been promulgated in the synod itself.[4] The bishop, however, is not obliged by the Code to promulgate his synodal decrees during the synod itself; rather, he can use any method of promulgation which he desires to use. Most likely the methods mentioned above for the promulgation of extra-synodal episcopal legislation could also be used in the case of synodal legislation. One practical method of promulgation, if the decrees are not promulgated in the sessions of the synod, would be the promulgation through their publication in book form to be distributed to the clergy. In a similar way it appears that those decrees which directly pertain to the laity could be published in pamphlet form to be distributed to them.

The law of canon 362 applies also to synods when held in a vicariate apostolic.[5]

---

[4] *Synodus Dioecesana Fargensis Prima* (Milwauchiae: Bruce, 1941), p. ix.
[5] Canon 304, §2.

Conclusions

As a result of this study the following conclusions are offered:

PART ONE

1. Although it is true that laws are instituted when they are promulgated, still the institution of a law is not the same as the promulgation of a law.

2. Since the Code of Canon Law states that laws are instituted when they are promulgated, a law must begin to bind, at least objectively (*in actu primo*), as soon as it has been adequately promulgated. When the legislator grants a period of time during which the subjects are not bound to obey the law (*vacatio legis*), the law binds *in actu primo* as soon as it has been promulgated. There can be no subjective obligation (*in actu secundo*) during the period of the *vacatio legis*. After the period of the quiescence of the law has elapsed, the subjective obligation begins for those who have become acquainted with the law or who, if unacquainted with it, are to be held accountable for their culpable negligence in not knowing the law.

3. At the present time no one denies the necessity of the element of promulgation for the existence of a law, but there is a sharp difference of opinion among authors concerning the degree of the necessity of the law's promulgation. It is evident that, although both groups offer an adequate explanation of the relation of promulgation to the notion of law, neither group is able to prove conclusively that their opinion is to be held to the exclusion of the other. At first the opinion which holds that the element of the promulgation of a law pertains to the essence of a law was the more common one. During the past century, however, and especially since the Code, the opposite opinion—that the element of promulgation is merely a necessary condition for the existence of a law—has become the more popular opinion. However, in consideration of the nature of law and in the light of the explanation given by modern authors, who distinguish

between an active and a passive promulgation, it seems that the element of promulgation does pertain to the essence of law. It is this opinion that appeals to the writer as the one to be preferred.

PART TWO

4. The use of two types of promulgation predominated in the early Church: a. Promulgation through letters carried by messengers to the individual bishops along with instructions that the latter look to the publication of the law in their dioceses, and b. Promulgation in the sessions of a council or a synod.

5. Pope Martin IV, in the year 1281, introduced a new method for the promulgation of pontifical legislation, and this method was the one in common use from 1281 until the twentieth century. Universal papal legislation was promulgated by means of a public posting of copies of the text of the law in the city of Rome.

6. Soon after the introduction of the method which was the one in common use after 1281 there arose a difference of opinion among the authors regarding the universal binding power of a law when it had been promulgated exclusively in the city of Rome. In the beginning the opinion which insisted that a papal law had also to be promulgated in every diocese if it was to achieve a universally binding force enjoyed some degree of probability, but it never gained the fuller measure of probability that attached to the opposite opinion. In fact, after the end of the eighteenth century it received little if any support from canonists. With the issuance of the Constitution *Promulgandi* on September 29, 1908, the controversy lapsed entirely from existence.

Bibliography

Sources

Acta Apostolicae Sedis, Commentarium Officiale, Romae, 1909 —.

Acta et Decreta Concilii Plenarii Baltimorensis Tertii, A.D. MDCCCXXXIV, Baltimorae: John Murphy, 1886.

Acta et Decreta Concilii Provincialis Mechliniensis Quarti anno MCMXX Mechliniae Habiti, Mechliniae: H. Dessain, 1923.

Acta et Decreta Concilii Provincialis Portlandensis in Oregon Quarti, anno 1932, Portland, Oregon: Sentinel Printery, 1934.

Acta et Decreta Concilii Provincialis Torontini Secundi, Toronto, 1938.

Acta et Decreta Sacrorum Conciliorum Recentiorum, Collectio Lacensis, 7 vols., Friburgi Brisgoviae, 1870-1890.

Acta Sanctae Sedis, 41 vols., Romae, 1865-1908.

Augustinus, Antonius, *Antiquae Decretalium Collectiones Commentariis et Emendationibus Illustratae,* Parisiis, 1621.

Benedicti XIV, Pont. Opt. Max. olim Prosper Cardinalis De Lambertinis Bullarium, 3 vols. in 4, Prati, 1845-1847.

Bullarii Romani Continuatio Summorum Pontificum, 9 vols. in 12, Prati, 1835-1856.

Bullarum Diplomatum et Privilegiorum Sanctorum Romanorum Pontificum Taurinensis Editio, 24 vols. et Appendix, Augustae Taurinorum—Neapoli, 1857-1872.

Codex Iuris Canonici Pii X Pontificis Maximi iussu digestus Benedicti Papae XV auctoritate promulgatus, Romae: Typis Polyglottis Vaticanis, 1917.

Codicis Iuris Canonici Fontes, cura Emi Petri Card. Gasparri editi, 9 vols., Romae (postea Civitate Vaticana): Typis Polyglottis Vaticanis, 1923-1939. (Vols. VII-IX, ed. cura et studio Emi Iustiniani Card. Serédi.)

Constitutiones Dioecesanae Brooklynienses, New York: Loughlin Bros., 1926.

Corpus Iuris Canonici, ed. Lipsien. 2., post Aemilii Ludovici Richteri curas instruxit Aemilius Friedberg, 2 vols., Lipsiae: Ex Officina Bernhardi Tauchnitz, 1879-1881. Editio anastatice repetita, Lipsiae: Tauchnitz, 1922.

Corpus Iuris Civilis, Vol. III, ed. stereotypa quinta, *Novellae,* quas recognovit Rudolfus Schoell, absolvit Guglielmus Kroll, Berolini: Apud Weidmannos, 1928.

Decretales D. Gregorii Papae IX suae integritati una cum glossis restitutae, cum privilegio Gregorii XIII, Pont. Max., et aliorum Principum, Romae, 1582.

Decretum Gratiani emendatum et notationibus illustratum una cum glossis, Gregorii XIII, Pont. Max., iussu editum, 2 vols., Romae, 1582.

Hardouin, Jean, *Acta Conciliorum et Epistolae Decretales ac Constitutiones Summorum Pontificum,* 12 vols., Parisiis, 1714-1715.

Jaffé, Philippus, *Regesta Pontificum Romanorum ab condita Ecclesia ad annum post Christum natum MCXCVIII,* 2.ed., correctam et auctam auspiciis Guglielmi Wattenbach, curaverunt F. Kaltenbrunner, P. Ewald, S. Loewenfeld, 2 vols. in 1, Lipsiae, 1885-1888.

Leonis XIII Pontificis Maximi Acta, 23 vols., Romae, 1881-1905.

Mansi, Joannes, *Sacrorum Conciliorum Nova et Amplissima Collectio,* 53 vols. in 60, Parisiis, 1901-1927.

Ninth Synod of the Diocese of Harrisburg, Harrisburg, 1944.

Pii X Pontificis Maximi Acta, 5 vols., Romae, 1905-1913.

Potthast, A., *Regesta Pontificum Romanorum inde ab anno post Christum natum MCXCVIII ad annum MCCCIV,* 2 vols., Berolini, 1874-1875.

Schroeder, H. J., *Canons and Decrees of the Council of Trent: Original Text with English Translation,* St. Louis: Herder, 1941.

Synodus Dioecesana Fargensis Prima, Milwauchiae: Bruce, 1941.

Reference Works

Allen, Carlton Kemp, *Law in the Making,* Oxford: Oxford University Press, 1927.

Alphonsus Maria de Ligorio, S., *Theologia Moralis,* ed. nova cura et studio P. Leonardi Gaudé, 4 vols., Romae, 1905-1912.

Altessera, Antonius Dadinus, *Opera Omnia,* Vol. X, *Commentarius in Singulas Decretales Innocentii III quae per libros Quinque Decretalium sparsae sunt,* Neapoli, 1780.

Aquinas, S. Thomas, *Summa Theologica,* ed. Marietti, 6 vols., Taurini Romae: Marietti, 1937.

Ayrinhac, H. A.—Lydon, P. J., *Penal Legislation in the New Code of Canon Law,* revised edition, New York: Benziger, 1944.

Ballerini, Antonius, *Opus Theologicum Morale,* Absolvit et edidit Dominicus Palmieri, 7 vols., Prati, 1889-1893.

Barbosa, Augustinus, *Collectanea Doctorum tam veterum quam recentiorum in Ius Pontificium Universum,* 6 vols., Lugduni, 1669.

Berutti, Christopher, *Institutiones Iuris Canonici,* 6 vols., Vol. I, Taurini-Romae: Marietti, 1936.

Beste, Udalricus, *Introductio in Codicem,* 2.ed., Collegeville: Saint John's Abbey Press, 1944.

Billuart, Carolus, *Summa Summae S. Thomae,* 6 vols., Leodii, 1754.

Bonacina, Martinus, *Opera Omnia,* ed. postrema, 3 vols., Venetiis, 1687.

Bouix, D., *Tractatus de Curia Romana,* Parisiis, 1859.

——, *Tractatus de Principiis Juris Canonici,* 2.ed., Parisiis.

Bouquillon, Thomas, *Theologia Moralis Fundamentalis,* 2.ed., Brugis, 1890.

Cappello, Felix, *Summa Iuris Canonici,* 3 vols., Romae: Apud Aedes Universitatis Gregorianae, 1938-1940 (Vol. I, 3.ed., 1938; Vol. II, 3.ed., 1939; Vol. III, 2.ed., 1940).

Cappello, Felix, *Tractatus Canonico-Moralis de Censuris,* 3.ed., Taurinorum Augustae: Marietti, 1933.

Castropalao, Ferdinandus de, *Opera Omnia,* 7 vols., Lugduni, 1700.

Chelodi, Ioannes, *Ius Canonicum de Delictis et Poenis et de Iudiciis Criminalibus,* 5.ed., recognita et aucta a Pio Ciprotti, Vicenza: Societá Anonima Tipografica, 1943.

——, *Ius Canonicum de Personis,* 3.ed., curavit Pius Ciprotti, Vicenza: Societá Anonima Tipografica, 1942.

Cicognani, Amleto, *Canon Law,* authorized English version by O'Hara and Brennan, 2.ed., Philadelphia: Dolphin Press, 1935.

Cironius, Innocentius, *Opera in Jus Canonicum: Quinta Compilatio Epistolarum Honorii III Pont. Max.,* Tolosae, 1645.

Cocchi, Guidus, *Commentarium in Codicem Iuris Canonici,* 8 vols. in 5, Taurinorum Augustae: Marietti, 1930-1940. Lib. I, 2.ed., 1921.

Coffey, P., *Ontology,* New York: Peter Smith, 1938.

Coronata, Matthaeus Conte a, *Institutiones Iuris Canonici,* 2.ed., 5 vols., Vols. I-IV, 2.ed., 1939-1945; Vol. V, 1936, Taurini: Marietti.

D'Annibale, J., *Summula Theologiae Moralis,* 3.ed., 3 vols., Romae, 1892.

De Meester, Alphonsus, *Juris Canonici et Juris Canonico-Civilis Compendium,* ed. nová, 3 vols. in 4, Brugis: Desclée, De Brouwer, 1921-1928.

Devoti, Johannes, *Jus Canonicum Universum Publicum et Privatum,* 3 vols., Romae, 1837.

Dictionnaire de Théologie Catholique, 14 vols. in 23, Paris, 1903-1939.

Fagnanus, Prosper, *Commentaria in Quinque Libros Decretalium,* 5 vols. in 3, Venetiis, 1709-1729.

Ferraris, Lucius, *Bibliotheca Canonica, Iuridica, Moralis, Theologica, necnon Ascetica, Polemica, Rubristica, Historica,* 9 vols., Romae, 1885-1899.

Ferreres, Joannes, *Institutiones Canonicae,* 2.ed., 2 vols., Barcinone, 1920.

Gonet, Joannes, *Clypeus Theologiae Thomisticae,* 5 vols., Parisiis, 1876.

Gredt, Joseph, *Elementa Philosophiae Aristotelico-Thomisticae,* 7.ed., 2 vols., Friburgi Brisgoviae: Herder, 1937.

Guilfoyle, Merlin J., *Custom,* The Catholic University of America Canon Law Studies, n. 105, Washington, D. C.: The Catholic University of America, 1937.

Gury, Joannes, *Compendium Theologiae Moralis,* 2.ed., 2 vols., Romae, 1869.

Hefele, Carolus, and Leclercq, Henri, *Histoire des Conciles,* 10 vols. in 19, Paris, 1907-1938.

Hostiensis, Cardinalis (Henricus de Segusio), *Commentaria in Quinque Decretalium Libros,* 5 vols., Venetiis, 1581.

Jolowicz, H., *Historical Introduction to the Study of Roman Law,* Cambridge, 1932.

Leurenius, Petrus, *Jus Canonicum Universum,* 5 vols. in 3, Venetiis, 1729.

Lijdsman, Bernard, *Introductio in Jus Canonicum,* Hilversum in Hollandia: Sumptibus Societatis Editricis Pontificiae Anonymae, olim Paulus Brand, 1924-1929.

Marc, Clemens, *Institutiones Morales Alphonsianae,* 2 vols., Romae, 1885.

Maroto, Philippus, *Institutiones Iuris Canonici,* 2 vols., Vol. I, 3.ed., Romae, 1921.

Merkelbach, Benedictus, *Summa Theologia Moralis ad Mentem D. Thomae et ad Normam Iuris Novi,* 3.ed., 3 vols., Parisiis: Desclée, 1938.

Michiels, Gommarus, *Normae Generales Juris Canonici,* 2 vols., Lublin: Universitas Catholica, 1929.

Migne, J. P., *Patrologiae Cursus Completus, Series Latina,* 221 vols. Parisiis, 1844-1864.

Mueller, O., *Sexti Pompeii Festi de Verborum Significatione quae supersunt,* Lipsiae, 1839.

Navarrus, Martinus, *Opera Omnia,* 6 vols., Venetiis, 1618.

Noel, Franciscus, *Theologiae R.P. Fr. Suarez Summa seu Compendium,* 4 vols., Parisiis, 1888.

Ojetti, B., *Commentarium in Codicem Iuris Canonici,* 4 vols., Romae: Apud Aedes Universitatis Gregorianae, 1927-1931.

Panormitanus, Abbas (Nicholaus de Tudeschis), *Commentaria in Quinque Libros Decretalium,* 5 vols. in 7, Venetiis, 1588.

Pichler, Vitus, *Candidatus Jurisprudentiae Sacrae,* 4.ed., 5 vols. Augustae Vindelicorum, 1733.

Pirhing, Ernricus, *Jus Canonicum in V Libros Decretalium,* ed. novissima, 4 vols., Dilingae, 1722.

Prümmer, Dominicus, *Manuale Theologiae Moralis,* 5.ed., 3 vols., Friburgi Brisgoviae: Herder, 1928.

Raus, J. B., *Institutiones Canonicae,* 2.ed., Lugduni-Parisiis: Typis Emmanuelis Vitte, 1931.

Regatillo, Eduardus, *Institutiones Iuris Canonici,* 2 vols., Santander: Sal Terrae, Vol. I, 2.ed., 1946, Vol. II, 1942.

Reiffenstuel, Anacletus, *Jus Canonicum Universum,* 5 vols. in 7, Parisiis, 1864-1870.

Rodrigo, Lucius, *Praelectiones Theologico-Morales Comillenses,* Tomus II, *Tractatus de Legibus,* Santander: Sal Terrae, 1944.

Roelker, Edward, *The Principles of Privilege according to the Code of Canon Law,* The Catholic University of America Canon Law Studies, n. 35, Washington, D. C.: The Catholic University of America, 1926.

Salmanticenses, *Cursus Theologiae Moralis,* 4 vols., Venetiis, 1714-1715.

——, *Cursus Theologicus,* 20 vols., Genève, 1870-1883.

Santi, Franciscus, *Praelectiones Juris Canonici,* 5 vols. in 2, New York, 1886.

Schmalzgrueber, Franciscus, *Jus Ecclesiasticum Universum,* 5 vols. in 12, Romae, 1843-1845.

Schmidt, John R., *The Principles of Authentic Interpretation in Canon 17 of the Code of Canon Law,* The Catholic University of American Canon Law Studies, n. 141, Washington, D. C.: The Catholic University of America Press, 1941.

Schroeder, H. J., *Disciplinary Decrees of the General Councils,* St. Louis: Herder, 1937.

Sipos, Stephanus, *Enchiridion Iuris Canonici,* Pécs: Ex Typographia "Haladás R. T.," 1926.

Sole, Iacobus, *De Delictis et Poenis,* Romae: Pustet, 1920.

Suarez, Franciscus, *Opera Omnia,* 28 vols., ed. Vivés, Parisiis, 1856-1861. Vols. V-VI, *De Legibus et Legislatore Deo.*

Sylvius, Franciscus, *Commentarium in Summam Theologicam S. Thomae Aquinatis,* ed., novissima, 4 vols., Venetiis, 1726.

Toso, A., *Ad Codicem Iuris Canonici Commentaria Minora,* 5 vols., Vol. I, Tiferni Tiberini: ex Offic. Typogr. Vinciana, 1921.

Van Espen, Zegerus, *Scripta Omnia,* 4 vols., Lovanii, 1753.

Van Hove, A., *Commentarium Lovaniense in Codicem Iuris Canonici,* Vol. I, Tom. II, *De Legibus Ecclesiasticis,* Mechliniae et Romae: Dessain, 1930.

——, *Commentarium Lovaniense in Codicem Iuris Canonici,* Vol. I, Tom. I, *Prolegomena,* 2.ed., Mechliniae et Romae: H. Dessain, 1945.

Vasquez, Gabriel, *Commentariorum ac Disputationum in Primam Secundae Sancti Thomae Tomus Secundus* ed. novissima, 2 vols., Lugduni, 1631.

Vecchiotti, Septimius, *Institutiones Canonicae,* 16.ed., 3 vols., Augustae Taurinorum, 1875.

Vermeersch, Arturus, *Theologiae Moralis Principia—Responsa—Consilia,* 4 vols., Vol. I, 3.ed., Roma: Pont. Univ. Gregoriana, 1933.

Vermeersch, Arturus-Creusen, Josephus, *Epitome Iuris Canonici,* 2.ed., 3 vols., Mechliniae-Romae: Dessain, 1923-1925.

Wernz, Franciscus, *Ius Decretalium,* 2.ed., 6 vols., Romae et Prati, 1906-1913.

Wernz, Franciscus-Vidal, Petrus, *Ius Canonicum,* 7 vols. in 8, Romae: Apud Aedes Universitatis Gregorianae, 1923-1938. Vol. I, 1938; Vol. VII, 1937.

Zaccaria, Franciscus A., *De Rebus ad Historiam atque Antiquitates Ecclesiae Pertinentibus Dissertationes Latinae,* 4 vols., Fulginiae, 1781, Vol. II, Diss. XI, *De Varia Ecclesiae praesertim Latinae in Sacris promulgandis Constitutionibus Disciplina.*

Zallinger, J. A., *Institutiones Juris Ecclesiastici,* 5 vols., Romae, 1823.

Articles

Creagh, John, "The Promulgation of Pontifical Law"—*The Catholic University Bulletin,* XV (1909), 23-41.

Gillet, P., "De lege data et nondum promulgata,"—*Jus Pontificium,* VIII (1928), 216-218.

Kuttner, S., "The Father of the Science of Canon Law,"—*The Jurist,* I (1941), 2-19.

Silva-Tarouca, C., "Nuovi studi sulle antiche lettere dei papi,"—*Gregorianum,* XII (1931), 349-425.

Periodicals

Catholic Telegraph-Register, The, Cincinnati, 1831 —.

Catholic University Bulletin, Washington, D. C., 1895 —.

Civiltà Cattolica, La, Romae, 1850 —.

Gregorianum, Romae, 1920 —.

Jus Pontificium, Romae, 1921 —.

Jurist, The, Washington, 1941 —.

Abbreviations

AAS—Acta Apostolicae Sedis.

ASS—Acta Sanctae Sedis.

Coll. Lac.—Collectio Lacensis.

Fontes—Codicis Iuris Canonici Fontes cura . . . Gasparri editi.

Mansi—*Sacrorum Conciliorum Nova et Amplissima Collectio.*

MPL—Migne, *Patrologia Latina.*

N.—Novella.

Alphabetical Index

Biographical Note

Martin N. Lohmuller was born on August 21, 1919, in Philadelphia, Pennsylvania. He attended Saint Henry's Parochial School and the Northeast Catholic High School for Boys. On September 2, 1935, he entered Saint Charles' Seminary, Overbrook, Pa., where he received the degree of Bachelor of Arts in 1942. He was ordained to the priesthood on June 3, 1944. The following October he entered the Catholic University of America to pursue graduate studies in the School of Canon Law. He received the Baccalaureate in Canon Law in May, 1945, and the degree of the Licentiate in Canon Law in June, 1946.

CANON LAW STUDIES*

1. FRERIKS, REV. CELESTINE A., C.PP.S., J.C.D., Religious Congregations in Their External Relations, 121 pp., 1916.
2. GALLIHER, REV. DANIEL M., O.P., J.C.D., Canonical Elections, 117 pp., 1917.
3. BORKOWSKI, REV. AURELIUS L., O.F.M., J.C.D., De Confraternitatibus Ecclesiasticis, 136 pp., 1918.
4. CASTILLO, REV. CAYO, J.C.D., Disertacion Historico-Canonica sobre la Potestad del Cabildo en Sede Vacante o Impedida del Vicario Capitular, 99 pp., 1919 (1918).
5. KUBELBECK, REV. WILLIAM J., S.T.B., J.C.D., The Sacred Penitentiaria and Its Relation to Faculties of Ordinaries and Priests, 129 pp., 1918.
6. PETROVITS, REV. JOSEPH, J.C., S.T.D., J.C.D., The New Church Law on Matrimony, X-461 pp., 1919.
7. HICKEY, REV. JOHN J., S.T.B., J.C.D., Irregularities and Simple Impediments in the New Code of Canon Law, 100 pp., 1920.
8. KLEKOTKA, REV. PETER J., S.T.B., J.C.D., Diocesan Consultors, 179 pp., 1920.
9. WANENMACHER, REV. FRANCIS, J.C.D., The Evidence in Ecclesiastical Procedure Affecting the Marriage Bond, 1920 (Printed 1935).
10. GOLDEN, REV. HENRY FRANCIS, J.C.D., Parochial Benefices in the New Code, IV-119 pp., 1921 (Printed 1925).
11. KOUDELKA, REV. CHARLES J., J.C.D., Pastors, Their Rights and Duties According to the New Code of Canon Law, 211 pp., 1921.
12. MELO, REV. ANTONIUS, O.F.M., J.C.D., De Exemptione Regularium, X-188 pp., 1921.
13. SCHAAF, REV. VALENTINE THEODORE, O.F.M., S.T.B., J.C.D., The Cloister, X-180 pp., 1921.
14. BURKE, REV. THOMAS JOSEPH, S.T.D., J.C.D., Competence in Ecclesiastical Tribunals, IV-117 pp., 1922.
15. LEECH, REV. GEORGE LEO, J.C.D., A Comparative Study of the Constitution "Apostolicae Sedis" and the "Codex Juris Canonici," 179 pp., 1922.
16. MOTRY, REV. HUBERT LOUIS, S.T.D., J.C.D., Diocesan Faculties According to the Code of Canon Law, II-167 pp., 1922.
17. MURPHY, REV. GEORGE LAWRENCE, J.C.D., Delinquencies and Penalties in the Administration and the Reception of the Sacraments, IV-121 pp., 1923.
18. O'REILLY, REV. JOHN ANTHONY, S.T.B., J.C.D., Ecclesiastical Sepulture in the New Code of Canon Law, II-129 pp., 1923.

* From nn. 1-100 only n. 25 is still obtainable. From n. 101 onward all numbers are available except the following: 101-114, also 116, 118, 120 and 122.

19. Michalicka, Rev. Wenceslas Cyrill, O.S.B., J.C.D., Judicial Procedure in Dismissal of Clerical Exempt Religious, 107 pp., 1923.
20. Dargin, Rev. Edward Vincent, S.T.B., J.C.D., Reserved Cases According to the Code of Canon Law, IV-103 pp., 1924.
21. Godfrey, Rev. John A., S.T.B., J.C.D., The Right of Patronage According to the Code of Canon Law, 153 pp., 1924.
22. Hagedorn, Rev. Francis Edward, J.C.D., General Legislation on Indulgences, II-154 pp., 1924.
23. King, Rev. James Ignatius, J.C.D., The Administration of the Sacraments to Dying Non-Catholics, V-141 pp., 1924.
24. Winslow, Rev. Francis Joseph, O.F.M., J.C.D., Vicars and Prefects Apostolic, IV-149 pp., 1924.
25. Correa, Rev. Jose Servelion, S.T.L., J.C.D., La Potestad Legislativa de la Iglesia Catolica, IV-127 pp., 1925.
26. Dugan, Rev. Henry Francis, A.M., J.C.D., The Judiciary Department of the Diocesan Curia, 87 pp., 1925.
27. Keller, Rev. Charles Frederick, S.T.B., J.C.D., Mass Stipends, 167 pp., 1925.
28. Paschang, Rev. John Linus, J.C.D., The Sacramentals According to the Code of Canon Law, 129 pp., 1925.
29. Piontek, Rev. Cyrillus, O.F.M., S.T.B., J.C.D., De Indulto Exclaustrationis necnon Saecularizationis, XIII-289 pp., 1925.
30. Kearney, Rev. Richard Joseph, S.T.B., J.C.D., Sponsors at Baptism According to the Code of Canon Law, IV-127 pp., 1925.
31. Bartlett, Rev. Chester Joseph, A.M., LL.B., J.C.D., The Tenure of Parochial Property in the United States of America, V-108 pp., 1926.
32. Kilker, Rev. Adrian Jerome, J.C.D., Extreme Unction, V-425 pp., 1926.
33. McCormick, Rev. Robert Emmett, J.C.D., Confessors of Religious, VIII-266 pp., 1926.
34. Miller, Rev. Newton Thomas, J.C.D., Founded Masses According to the Code of Canon Law, VII-93 pp., 1926.
35. Roelker, Rev. Edward G., S.T.D., J.C.D., Principles of Privilege According to the Code of Canon Law, XI-166 pp., 1926.
36. Bakalarczyk, Rev. Richardus, M.I.C., J.U.D., De Novitiatu, VIII-208 pp., 1927.
37. Pizzuti, Rev. Lawrence, O.F.M., J.U.L., De Parochis Religiosis, 1927. (Not Printed.)
38. Bliley, Rev. Nicholas Martin, O.S.B., J.C.D., Altars According to the Code of Canon Law, XIX-132 pp., 1927.
39. Brown, Mr. Brendan Francis, A.B., LL.M., J.U.D., The Canonical Juristic Personality with Special Reference to its Status in the United States of America, V-212 pp., 1927.
40. Cavanaugh, Rev. William Thomas, C.P., J.U.D., The Reservation of the Blessed Sacrament, VIII-101 pp., 1927.
41. Doheny, Rev. William J., C.S.C., A.B., J.U.D., Church Property: Modes of Acquisition, X-118 pp., 1927.

42. FELDHAUS, REV. ALOYSIUS H., C.PP.S., J.C.D., Oratories, IX-141 pp., 1927.
43. KELLY, REV. JAMES PATRICK, A.B., J.C.D., The Jurisdiction of the Simple Confessor, X-208 pp., 1927..
44. NEUBERGER, REV. NICHOLAS J., J.C.D., Canon 6 or the Relation of the Codex Juris Canonici to the Preceding Legislation, V-95 pp., 1927.
45. O'KEEFE, REV. GERALD MICHAEL, J.C.D., Matrimonial Dispensations, Powers of Bishops, Priests, and Confessors, VIII-232 pp., 1927.
46. QUIGLEY, REV. JOSEPH A. M., A.B., J.C.D., Condemned Societies, 139 pp., 1927.
47. ZAPLOTNIK, REV. JOHANNES LEO, J.C.D., De Vicariis Foraneis, X-142 pp., 1927.
48. DUSKIE, REV. JOHN ALOYSIUS, A.B., J.C.D., The Canonical Status of the Orientals in the United States, VIII-196 pp., 1928.
49. HYLAND, REV. FRANCIS EDWARD, J.C.D., Excommunication, Its Nature, Historical Development and Effects, VII-181 pp., 1928.
50. REINMANN, REV. GERALD JOSEPH, O.M.C., J.C.D., The Third Order Secular of Saint Francis, 201 pp., 1928.
51. SCHENK, REV. FRANCIS J., J.C.D., The Matrimonial Impediments of Mixed Religion and Disparity of Cult, XVI-318 pp., 1929.
52. COADY, REV. JOHN JOSEPH, S.T.D., J.U.D., A.M., The Appointment of Pastors, VIII-150 pp., 1929.
53. KAY, REV. THOMAS HENRY, J.C.D., Competence in Matrimonial Procedure, VIII-164 pp., 1929.
54. TURNER, REV. SIDNEY JOSEPH, C.P., J.U.D., The Vow of Poverty, XLIX-217 pp., 1929.
55. KEARNEY, REV. RAYMOND A., A.B., S.T.D., J.C.D., The Principles of Delegation, VII-149 pp., 1929.
56. CONRAN, REV. EDWARD JAMES, A.B., J.C.D., The Interdict, V-163 pp., 1930.
57. O'NEILL, REV. WILLIAM H., J.C.D., Papal Rescripts of Favor, VII-218 pp., 1930.
58. BASTNAGEL, REV. CLEMENT VINCENT, J.U.D., The Appointment of Parochial Adjutants and Assistants, XV-257 pp., 1930.
59. FERRY, REV. WILLIAM A., A.B., J.C.D., Stole Fees, V-136 pp., 1930.
60. COSTELLO, REV. JOHN MICHAEL, A.B., J.C.D., Domicile and Quasi-Domicile, VII-201 pp., 1930.
61. KREMER, REV. MICHAEL NICHOLAS, A.B., S.T.B., J.C.D., Church Support in the United States, VI-136 pp., 1930.
62. ANGULO, REV. LUIS, C.M., J.C.D., Legislation de la Iglesia sobre la intencion en la application de la Santa Misa, VII-104 pp., 1931.
63. FREY, REV. WOLFGANG NORBERT, O.S.B., A.B., J.C.D., The Act of Religious Profession, VIII-174 pp., 1931.
64. RÓBERTS, REV. JAMES BRENDAN, A.B., J.C.D., The Banns of Marriage, XIV-140 pp., 1931.
65. RYDER, REV. RAYMOND ALOYSIUS, A.B., J.C.D., Simony, IX-151 pp., 1931.

66. Campagna, Rev. Angelo, Ph.D., J.U.D., Il Vicario Generale del Vescovo, VII-205 pp., 1931.
67. Cox, Rev. Joseph Godfrey, A.B., J.C.D., The Administration of Seminaries, VI-124 pp., 1931.
68. Gregory, Rev. Donald J., J.U.D., The Pauline Privilege, XV-165 pp., 1931.
69. Donohue, Rev. John F., J.C.D., The Impediment of Crime, VII-110 pp., 1931.
70. Dooley, Rev. Eugene A., O.M.I., J.C.D., Church Law on Sacred Relics, IX-143 pp., 1931.
71. Orth, Rev. Clement Raymond, O.M.C., J.C.D., The Approbation of Religious Institutes, 171 pp., 1931.
72. Pernicone, Rev. Joseph M., A.B., J.C.D., The Ecclesiastical Prohibition of Books, XII-267 pp., 1932.
73. Clinton, Rev. Connell, A.B., J.C.D., The Paschal Precept, IX-108 pp., 1932.
74. Donnelly, Rev. Francis B., A.M., S.T.L., J.C.D., The Diocesan Synod, VIII-125 pp., 1932.
75. Torrente, Rev. Camilo, C.M.F., J.C.D., Las Procesiones Sagradas, V-145 pp., 1932.
76. Murphy, Rev. Edwin J., C.PP.S., J.C.D., Suspension Ex Informata Conscientia, XI-122 pp., 1932.
77. MacKenzie, Rev. Eric F., A.M., S.T.L., J.C.D., The Delict of Heresy in its Commission, Penalization, Absolution, VII-124 pp., 1932.
78. Lyons, Rev. Avitus E., S.T.B., J.C.D., The Collegiate Tribunal of First Instance, XI-147 pp., 1932.
79. Connolly, Rev. Thomas A., J.C.D., Appeals, XI-195 pp., 1932.
80. Sangmeister, Rev. Joseph V., A.B., J.C.D., Force and Fear as Precluding Matrimonial Consent, V-211 pp., 1932.
81. Jaeger, Rev. Leo A., A.B., J.C.D., The Administration of Vacant and Quasi-Vacant Episcopal Sees in the United States, IX-229 pp., 1932.
82. Rimlinger, Rev. Herbert T., J.C.D., Error Invalidating Matrimonial Consent, VII-79 pp., 1932.
83. Barrett, Rev. John D. M., S.S., J.C.D., A Comparative Study of the Councils of Baltimore and the Code of Canon Law, X-223 pp., 1932.
84. Carberry, Rev. John J., Ph.D., S.T.D., J.C.D., The Juridical Form of Marriage, X-177 pp., 1934.
85. Dolan, Rev. John L., A.B., J.C.D., The Defensor Vinculi, XII-157 pp., 1934.
86. Hannan, Rev. Jerome D., A.M., S.T.D., LL.B., J.C.D., The Canon Law of Wills, IX-517 pp., 1934.
87. Lemieux, Rev. Delise A., A.M., J.C.D., The Sentence in Ecclesiastical Procedure, IX-131 pp., 1934.
88. O'Rourke, Rev. James J., A.B., J.C.D., Parish Registers, VII-109 pp., 1934.
89. Timlin, Rev. Bartholomew, O.F.M., A.M., J.C.D., Conditional Matrimonial Consent, X-381 pp., 1934.

90. WAHL, REV. FRANCIS X., A.B., J.C.D., The Matrimonial Impediments of Consanguinity and Affinity, VI-125 pp., 1934.
91. WHITE, REV. ROBERT J., A.B., LL.B., S.T.B., J.C.D., Canonical Ante-Nuptial Promises and the Civil Law, VI-152 pp., 1934.
92. HERRERA, REV. ANTONIO PARRA, O.C.D., J.C.D., Legislacion Ecclesiastica sobra el Ayuno y la Abstinencia, XI-191 pp., 1935.
93. KENNEDY, REV. EDWIN J., J.C.D., The Special Matrimonial Process in Cases of Evident Nullity, X-165 pp., 1935.
94. MANNING, REV. JOHN J., A.B., J.C.D., Presumption of Law in Matrimonial Procedure, XI-111 pp., 1935.
95. MOEDER, REV. JOHN M., J.C.D., The Proper Bishop for Ordination and Dimissorial Letters, VII-135 pp., 1935.
96. O'MARA, REV. WILLIAM A., A.B., J.C.D., Canonical Causes for Matrimonial Dispensations, IX-155 pp., 1935.
97. REILLY, REV. PETER, J.C.D., Residence of Pastors, IX-81 pp., 1935.
98. SMITH, REV. MARINER T., O.P., S.T.Lr., J.C.D., The Penal Law for Religious, VIII-169 pp., 1935.
99. WHALEN, REV. DONALD W., A.M., J.C.D., The Value of Testimonial Evidence in Matrimonial Procedure, XIII-297 pp., 1935.
100. CLEARY, REV. JOSEPH F., J.C.D., Canonical Limitations on the Alienation of Church Property, VIII-141 pp., 1936.
101. GLYNN, REV. JOHN C., J.C.D., The Promoter of Justice, XX-337 pp., 1936.
102. BRENNAN, REV. JAMES H., S.S., M.A., S.T.B., J.C.D., The Simple Convalidation of Marriage, VI-135 pp., 1937.
103. BRUNINI, REV. JOSEPH BERNARD, J.C.D., The Clerical Obligations of Canons 139 and 142, X-121 pp., 1937.
104. CONNOR, REV. MAURICE, A.B., J.C.D., The Administrative Removal of Pastors, VIII-159 pp., 1937.
105. GUILFOYLE, REV. MERLIN JOSEPH, J.C.D., Custom, XI-144 pp., 1937.
106. HUGHES, REV. JAMES AUSTIN, A.B., A.M., J.C.D., Witnesses in Criminal Trials of Clerics, IX-140 pp., 1937.
107. JANSEN, REV. RAYMOND J., A.B., S.T.L., J.C.D., Canonical Provisions for Catechetical Instruction, VII-153 pp., 1937.
108. KEALY, REV. JOHN JAMES, A.B., J.C.D., The Introductory Libellus in Church Court Procedure, XI-121 pp., 1937.
109. MCMANUS, REV. JAMES EDWARD, C.SS.R., J.C.D., The Administration of Temporal Goods in Religious Institutes, XVI-196 pp., 1937.
110. MORIARITY, REV. EUGENE JAMES, J.C.D., Oaths in Ecclesiastical Courts, X-115 pp., 1937.
111. RAINER, REV. ELIGIUS GEORGE, C.SS.R., J.C.D., Suspension of Clerics, XVII-249 pp., 1937.
112. REILLY, REV. THOMAS F., C.SS.R., J.C.D., Visitation of Religious, VI-195 pp., 1938.
113. MORIARITY, REV. FRANCIS E., C.SS.R., J.C.D., The Extraordinary Absolution from Censures, XV-334 pp., 1938.
114. CONNOLLY, REV. NICHOLAS P., J.C.D., The Canonical Erection of Parishes, X-132 pp., 1938.

115. Donovan, Rev. James Joseph, J.C.D., The Pastor's Obligation in Prenuptial Investigation, XII-322 pp., 1938.

116. Harrigan, Rev. Robert J., M.A., S.T.B., J.C.D., The Radical Sanation of Invalid Marriages, VIII-208 pp., 1938.

117. Boffa, Rev. Conrad Humbert, J.C.D., Canonical Provisions for Catholic Schools, VII-211 pp., 1939.

118. Parsons, Rev. Anscar John, O.M.Cap., J.C.D., Canonical Elections, XII-236 pp., 1939.

119. Reilly, Rev. Edward Michael, A.B., J.C.D., The General Norms of Dispensation, XII-156 pp., 1939.

120. Ryan, Rev. Gerald Aloysius, A.B., J.C.D., Principles of Episcopal Jurisdiction, XII-172 pp., 1939.

121. Burton, Rev. Francis James, C.S.C., A.B., J.C.D., A Commentary on Canon 1125, X-222 pp., 1940.

122. Miaskiewicz, Rev. Francis Sigismund, J.C.D., Supplied Jurisdiction According to Canon 209, XII-340 pp., 1940.

123. Rice, Rev. Patrick William, A.B., J.C.D., Proof of Death in Prenuptial Investigation, VIII-156 pp., 1940.

124. Anglin, Rev. Thomas Francis, M.S., J.C.D., The Eucharistic Fast, VIII-183 pp., 1941.

125. Coleman, Rev. John Jerome, J.C.D., The Minister of Confirmation, VI-153 pp., 1941.

126. Downs, Rev. John Emmanuel, A.B., J.C.D., The Concept of Clerical Immunity, XI-163 pp., 1941.

127. Esswein, Rev. Anthony Albert, J.C.D., Extrajudicial Penal Powers of Ecclesiastical Superiors, X-144 pp., 1941.

128. Farrell, Rev. Benjamin Francis, M.A., S.T.L., J.C.D., The Rights and Duties of the Local Ordinary Regarding Congregations of Women Religious of Pontifical Approval, V-195 pp., 1941.

129. Feeney, Rev. Thomas John, A.B., S.T.L., J.C.D., Restitutio in Integrum, VI-169 pp., 1941.

130. Findlay, Rev. Stephen William, O.S.B., A.B., J.C.D., Canonical Norms Governing the Deposition and Degradation of Clerics, XVII-279 pp., 1941.

131. Goodwine, Rev. John, A.B., S.T.L., J.C.D., The Right of the Church to Acquire Property, VIII-119 pp., 1941.

132. Heston, Rev. Edward Louis, C.S.C., Ph.D., S.T.D., J.C.D., The Alienation of Church Property in the United States, XII-222 pp., 1941.

133. Hogan, Rev. James John, A.B., S.T.L., J.C.D., Judicial Advocates and Procurators, XIII-200 pp., 1941.

134. Kealy, Rev. Thomas M., A.B., Litt.B., J.C.D., Dowry of Women Religious, IX-152 pp., 1941.

135. Keene, Rev. Michael James, O.S.B., J.C.D., Religious Ordinaries and Canon 198, V-164 pp., 1942.

136. Kerin, Rev. Charles A., S.S., M.A., S.T.B., J.C.D., The Privation of Christian Burial, XVI-279 pp., 1941.

137. Louis, Rev. William Francis, M.A., J.C.D., Diocesan Archives, X-101 pp., 1941.
138. McDevitt, Rev. Gilbert Joseph, A.B., J.C.D., Legitimacy and Legitimation, X-247 pp., 1941.
139. McDonough, Rev. Thomas Joseph, A.B., J.C.D., Apostolic Administrators, X-217 pp., 1941.
140. Meier, Rev. Carl Anthony, A.B., J.C.D., Penal Administrative Procedure Against Negligent Pastors, XI-240 pp., 1941.
141. Schmidt, Rev. John Rogg, A.B., J.C.D., The Principles of Authentic Interpretation in Canon 17 of the Code of Canon Law, XII-331 pp., 1941.
142. Slafkosky, Rev. Andrew Leonard, A.B., J.C.D., The Canonical Episcopal Visitations of the Diocese, X-197 pp., 1941.
143. Swoboda, Rev. Innocent Robert, O.F.M., J.C.D., Ignorance in Relation to the Imputability of Delicts, IX-271 pp., 1941.
144. Dubé, Rev. Arthur Joseph, A.B., J.C.D., The General Principles for the Reckoning of Time in Canon Law, VIII-299 pp., 1941.
145. McBride, Rev. James T., A.B., J.C.D., Incardination and Excardination of Seculars, XX-585 pp., 1941.
146. Król, Rev. John T., J.C.D., The Defendant in Ecclesiastical Trials, XII-207 pp., 1942.
147. Comyns, Rev. Joseph J.,. C.SS.R., A.B., J.C.D., Papal and Episcopal Administration of Church Property, XIV-155 pp., 1942.
148. Barry, Rev. Garrett Francis, O.M.I., J.C.D., Violation of the Cloister, XII-260 pp., 1942.
149. Bolduc, Rev. Gatien, C.S.V., A.B., S.T.L., J.C.D., Les Études dans les Religions Cléricales, VIII-155 pp., 1942.
150. Boyle, Rev. David John, M.A., J.C.D., The Juridic Effects of Moral Certitude on Pre-Nuptial Guarantees, XII-188 pp., 1942.
151. Canavan, Rev. Walter Joseph, M.A., Litt.D., J.C.D., The Profession of Faith, XII-143 pp., 1942.
152. Desrochers, Rev. Bruno, A.B., Ph.L., S.T.B., J.C.D., Le Premier Concile Plénier de Québec et le Code de Droit Canonique, XIV-186 pp., 1942.
153. Dillon, Rev. Robert Edward, A.B., J.C.D., Common Law Marriage, X-148 pp., 1942.
154. Dodwell, Rev. Edward John, Ph.D., S.T.B., J.C.D., The Time and Place for the Celebration of Marriage, X-156 pp., 1942.
155. Donnellan, Rev. Thomas Andrew, A.B., J.C.D., The Obligation of the Missa pro Populo, VII-131 pp., 1942.
156. Eltz, Rev. Louis Anthony, A.B., J.C.D., Cooperation in Crime, XII-208 pp., 1942.
157. Gass, Rev. Sylvester Francis, M.A., J.C.D., Ecclesiastical Pensions, XI-206 pp., 1942.
158. Guiniven, Rev. John Joseph, C.SS.R., J.C.D., The Precept of Hearing Mass, XIV-188 pp., 1942.
159. Gulcynski, Rev. John Theophilus, J.C.D., The Desecration and Violation of Churches, X-126 pp., 1942.

160. Hammill, Rev. John Leo, M.A., J.C.D., The Obligations of the Traveler According to Canon 14, VIII-204 pp., 1942.
161. Haydt, Rev. John Joseph, A.B., J.C.D., Reserved Benefices, XI-148 pp., 1942.
162. Huser, Rev. Roger John, O.F.M., A.B., J.C.D., The Crime of Abortion in Canon Law, XII-187 pp., 1942.
163. Kearney, Rev. Francis Patrick, A.B., S.T.L., J.C.D., The Principles of Canon 1127, X-162 pp., 1942.
164. Linahen, Rev. Leo James, S.T.L., J.C.D., De Absolutione Complicis In Peccato Turpi, 114 pp., 1942.
165. McCloskey, Rev. Joseph Aloysius, A.B., J.C.D., The Subject of Ecclesiastical Law According to Canon 12, XVII-246 pp., 1942.
166. O'Neill, Rev. Francis Joseph, C.SS.R., J.C.D., The Dismissal of Religious in Temporary Vows, XIII-220 pp., 1942.
167. Prince, Rev. John Edward, A.B., S.T.B., J.C.D., The Diocesan Chancellor, X-136 pp., 1942.
168. Riesner, Rev. Albert Joseph, C.SS.R., J.C.D., Apostates and Fugitives from Religious Institutes, IX-168 pp., 1942.
169. Stenger, Rev. Joseph Bernard, J.C.D., The Mortgaging of Church Property, 186 pp., 1942.
170. Waldron, Rev. Joseph Francis, A.B., J.C.D., The Minister of Baptism, XII-197 pp., 1942.
171. Willett, Rev. Robert Albert, J.C.D., The Probative Value of Documents in Ecclesiastical Trials, X-124 pp., 1942.
172. Woeber, Rev. Edward Martin, M.A., J.C.D., The Interpellations, XII-161 pp., 1942.
173. Benko, Rev. Matthew Aloysius, O.S.B., M.A., J.C.D., The Abbot *Nullius*, XVI-148 pp., 1943.
174. Christ, Rev. Joseph James, M.A., S.T.L., J.C.D., Dispensation from Vindicative Penalties, XIII-285 pp., 1943.
175. Clancy, Rev. Patrick M. J., O.P., A.B., S.T.Lr., J.C.D., The Local Religious Superior, X-229 pp., 1943.
176. Clarke, Rev. Thomas James, J.C.D., Parish Societies, XII-147 pp., 1943.
177. Connolly, Rev. John Patrick, S.T.L., J.C.D., Synodal Examiners, and Parish Priest Consultors, X-223 pp., 1943.
178. Drumm, Rev. William Martin, A.B., J.C.D., Hospital Chaplains, XII-175 pp., 1943.
179. Flanagan, Rev. Bernard Joseph, A.B., S.T.L., J.C.D., The Canonical Erection of Religious Houses, X-147 pp., 1943.
180. Kelleher, Rev. Stephen Joseph, A.B., S.T.B., J.C.D., Discussions with Non-Catholics: Canonical Legislation, X-93 pp., 1943.
181. Lewis, Rev. Gordian, C.P., J.C.D., Chapters in Religious Institutes, XII-169 pp., 1943.
182. Marx, Rev. Adolph, J.C.D., The Declaration of Nullity of Marriages Contracted Outside the Church, X-151 pp., 1943.
183. Matulenas, Rev. Raymond Anthony, O.S.B., A.B., J.C.D., Communication, a Source of Privileges, XII-225 pp., 1943.

184. O'LEARY, REV. CHARLES GERARD, C.SS.R., J.C.D., Religious Dismissed After Perpetual Profession, X-213 pp., 1943.

185. POWER, REV. CORNELIUS MICHAEL, J.C.D., The Blessing of Cemeteries, XII-231 pp., 1943.

186. SHUHLER, REV. RALPH VINCENT, O.S.A., J.C.D., Privileges of Religious to Absolve and Dispense, XII-195 pp., 1943.

187. ZIOLKOWSKI, REV. THADDEUS STANISLAUS, A.B., J.C.D., The Consecration and Blessing of Churches, XII-151 pp., 1943.

188. HENEGHAN, REV. JOHN JOSEPH, S.T.D., J.C.D., The Marriages of Unworthy Catholics: Canons 1065 and 1066, XVI-213 pp., 1944.

189. CARROLL, REV. COLEMAN FRANCIS, M.A., S.T.L., J.C.L., Charitable Institutions.

190. CIESLUK, REV. JOSEPH EDWARD, PH.B., S.T.L., J.C.L., National Parishes in the United States.

191. COBURN, REV. VINCENT PAUL, A.B., J.C.D., Marriages of Conscience, XII-172 pp., 1944.

192. CONNORS, REV. CHARLES PAUL, C.S.SP., A.B., J.C.D., Extra-Judicial Procurators in the Code of Canon Law, X-94 pp., 1944.

193. COYLE, REV. PAUL RAYMOND, A.B., J.C.D., Judicial Exceptions, IX-142 pp., 1944.

194. FAIR, REV. BARTHOLOMEW FRANCIS, A.B., S.T.L., J.C.D., The Impediment of Abduction, XII-122 pp., 1944.

195. GALLAGHER, REV. THOMAS RAPHAEL, O.P., A.B., S.T.LR., J.C.D., The Examination of the Qualities of the Ordinand, X-166 pp., 1944.

196. GANNON, REV. JOHN MARK, S.T.L., J.C.D., The Interstices Required for the Promotion to Orders, VII-100 pp., 1944.

197. GOLDSMITH, REV. J. WILLIAM, B.C.S., S.T.L., J.C.D., The Competence of Church and State Over Marriage—Disputed Points, X-128 pp., 1944.

198. GOODWINE, REV. JOSEPH GERARD, A.B., S.T.B., J.C.D., The Reception of Converts, XIV-326 pp., 1944.

199. KOWALSKI, REV. ROMUALD EUGENE, O.F.M., A.B., J.C.D., Sustenance of Religious Houses of Regulars, X-174 pp., 1944.

200. MCCOY, REV. ALAN EDWARD, O.F.M., J.C.D., Force and Fear in Relation to Delictual Imputability and Penal Responsibility, XII-160 pp., 1944.

201. MCDEVITT, REV. VINCENT JOHN, PH.B., S.T.L., J.C.L., Perjury.

202. MARTIN, REV. THOMAS OWEN, PH.D., S.T.D., J.C.D., Adverse Possession, Prescription and Limitation of Actions: The Canonical "Praescriptio," XX-208 pp., 1944.

203. MIKLOSOVIC, REV. PAUL JOHN, A.B., J.C.L., Attempted Marriages and Their Consequent Juridic Effects.

204. MUNDY, REV. THOMAS MAURICE, A.B., S.T.L., J.C.D., The Union of Parishes, X-164 pp., 1944.

205. O'DEA, REV. JOHN COYLE, A.B., J.C.D., The Matrimonial Impediment of Nonage, VIII-126 pp., 1944.

206. OLALIA, REV. ALEXANDER AYSON, S.T.L., J.C.D., A Comparative Study of the Christian Constitution of States and the Constitution of the Philippine Commonwealth, XII-136 pp., 1944.
207. POISSON, REV. PIERRE-MARIE, C.S.C., A.B., PH.L., THL., J.C.L., Droits Patrimoniaux des Maisons et des Eglises Religieuses.
208. STADALNIKAS, REV. CASIMIR JOSEPH, M.I.C., J.C.D., Reservation of Censures, X-141 pp., 1944.
209. SULLIVAN, REV. EUGENE HENRY, S.T.L., J.C.D., Proof of the Reception of the Sacraments, X-165 pp., 1944.
210. VAUGHAN, REV. WILLIAM EDWARD, J.C.D., Constitutions for Diocesan Courts, X-210 pp., 1944.
211. PARO, REV. GINO, S.T.D., J.C.L., The Right of Apostolic Delegation.
212. BALZER, REV. RALPH FRANCIS, C.P., J.C.D., The Computation of Time in a Canonical Novitiate, X-227 pp., 1945.
213. DOUGHERTY, REV. JOHN WHELAN, A.B., S.T.L., J.C.D., De Inquisitione Speciali, XII-195 pp., 1945.
214. DZIOB, REV. MICHAEL WALTER, J.C.D., The Sacred Congregation for the Oriental Church, XII-181 pp., 1945.
215. EIDENSCHINK, REV. JOHN ALBERT, O.S.B., B.A., J.C.D., The Election of Bishops in the Letters of Pope Gregory the Great, VII-200 pp., 1945.
216. GILL, REV. NICHOLAS, C.P., J.C.D., The Spiritual Prefect in Clerical Religious Houses of Study, X-140 pp., 1945.
217. HYNES, REV. HARRY GERARD, S.T.L., J.C.D., The Privileges of Cardinals, XII-183 pp., 1945.
218. MCDEVITT, REV. GERALD VINCENT, S.T.L., J.C.D., The Renunciation of an Ecclesiastical Office, XIV-179 pp., 1945.
219. MANNING, REV. JOSEPH LEROY, J.C.D., The Free Conferral of Offices, VIII-116 pp., 1945.
220. MEYER, REV. LOUIS G., O.S.B., A.B., S.T.B., J.C.D., Alms-gathering by Religious, XII-163 pp., 1945.
221. O'DONNELL, REV. CLETUS FRANCIS, M.A., J.C.D., The Marriage of Minors, XII-268 pp., 1945.
222. PRUNSKIS, REV. JOSEPH, J.C.D., Comparative Law, Ecclesiastical and Civil, in Lithuanian Concordat, X-161 pp., 1945.
223. SWEENEY, REV. FRANCIS PATRICK, C.SS.R., J.C.D., The Reduction of Clerics to the Lay State, X-199 pp., 1945.
224. VOGELPOHL, REV. HENRY JOHN, J.C.D., The Simple Impediments to Holy Orders, XVI-190 pp., 1945.
225. BROCKHAUS, REV. THOMAS AQUINAS, O.S.B., J.C.D., Religious who are known as *Conversi*, X-127 pp., 1945.
226. GRIESE, REV. N. ORVILLE, S.T.D., J.C.D., The Marriage Contract and the Procreation of Offspring, XVI-224 pp., 1946.

227. Boudreaux, Rev. Warren Louis, J.C.L., The "*ab acatholicis nati*" of Canon 1099, § 2.
228. Bowe, Rev. Thomas Joseph, A.B., J.C.L., Religious Superioresses.
229. Diederichs, Rev. Michael Ferdinand, S.C.J., J.C.D., The Jurisdiction of the Latin Ordinaries over their Oriental Subjects, XIV-153 pp., 1946.
230. Dingman, Rev. Maurice John, A.B., S.T.L., J.C.L., The Plaintiff in Contentious Trials.
231. Frison, Rev. Basil, C.M.F., M.Mus., J.C.D., The Retroactivity of Law, X-221 pp., 1946.
232. Galvin, Rev. William Anthony, M.A., J.C.D., The Administrative Transfer of Pastors, XII-288 pp., 1946.
233. Goracy, Rev. Joseph C., J.C.L., The Diriment Matrimonial Impediment of Major Orders.
234. Hale, Rev. Joseph Francis, M.A., S.T.L., J.C.L., The Pastor of Burial.
235. Henry, Rev. Joseph Arthur, A.B., J.C.D., The Mass and Holy Communion: Inter-Ritual Law, XII-138 pp., 1946.
236. Linenberger, Rev. Herbert, C.PP.S., J.C.L., The False Denunciation of an Innocent Confessor.
237. Lowry, Rev. James Martin, A.B., J.C.L., Dispensation from Private Vows.
238. Lynch, Rev. George Edward, A.B., S.T.L., J.C.D., Coadjutors and Auxiliaries of Bishops, X-107 pp., 1947.
239. Lynch, Rev. Timothy, M.S.SS.T., J.C.L., Contracts between Bishops and Religious Congregations.
240. McClunn, Rev. Justin David, A.B., S.T.L., J.C.D., Administrative Recourse, VII-142 pp., 1946.
241. Lohmuller, Rev. Martin Nicholas, A.B., J.C.L., The Promulgation of Law.
242. McGrath, Rev. James, A.B., J.C.D., The Privilege of the Canon, XII-156 pp., 1946.
243. Marbach, Rev. Joseph Francis, A.B., J.C.D., Marriage Legislation for the Catholics of the Oriental Rites in the United States and Canada, XIV-314 pp., 1946.
244. Shimkus, Rev. Bernard Aloysius, A.B., J.C.L., The Determination and Transfer of Rite.
245. Smith, Rev. Vincent Michael, A.B., S.T.L., J.C.L., Ignorance Affecting Matrimonial Consent.
246. Wachtrle, Rev. Paul Anthony, A.B., J.C.L., The Baptism of the Children of Non-Catholics.

www.ingramcontent.com/pod-product-compliance
Lightning Source LLC
LaVergne TN
LVHW050213080826
844660LV00012B/404

* 9 7 8 0 8 1 3 2 2 4 2 1 3 *